Watercolour by Sarah Hoare, showing Samuel Hoare at Heath House,
Hampstead, in an imaginary gallery hung with portraits of his friends

THE VOLUNTARY INSANE

Detail of the portrait of Crabbe, commissioned by his publisher
John Murray from Thomas Phillips RA, copied by Sarah Hoare for
her imaginary picture gallery

THE
VOLUNTARY
INSANE

by

GEORGE CRABBE

Edited by

FELIX PRYOR

Richard Cohen Books · London

British Library Cataloguing in Publication Data:
A catalogue record for this book is available from the British Library

Copyright © 1995 by Felix Pryor

ISBN 1 86066 025 8

First published in Great Britain in 1995 by
Richard Cohen Books
7 Manchester Square
London W1M 5RE

Typeset in Linotron 202 Fournier by
Rowland Phototypesetting Ltd,
Bury St Edmunds, Suffolk

Printed in Great Britain by
Biddles Ltd, Guildford

Contents

List of Illustrations

Acknowledgements

My first thanks are due to my father, the discoverer of the notebook, and to my brother for taking the photographs. Simon Rae has provided encouragement from an early stage, not least by agreeing to publish a foretaste of the poem in his magisterial *Faber Book of Murder* (lines 713–1040). I am grateful, too, to the late John G. Murray, for showing me the Crabbe notebooks in his firm's possession, and to Ian F. Lyle, Librarian, and Tina Craig of the Royal College of Surgeons, for showing me the leaf Sarah Hoare cut out of the notebook, now in the Hunter-Baillie Collection.

I am also most grateful to Andrew Barlow for his long, patient and meticulous work in transcribing the notebook; to Mary Sandys for her valuable suggestions and the spotting of several blunders, and to Christine Shuttleworth likewise. Biggest and best thanks must go to Richard Cohen, Georgina Laycock, Colin Nicholson, Margaret Fraser, Wendy Venis, Rebecca Swift and Patricia Chetwyn. Except, that is, for the bouquet I owe Julia Hamilton, to whom I would have offered the dedication, had it been in my gift.

TFMP

Introduction

The Voluntary Insane is here published for the first time. It is, I believe, George Crabbe's masterpiece.

It came to light in December 1989 in a notebook containing four long poems in Crabbe's handwriting. All were otherwise unknown, except for one published from an earlier draft in another notebook. All four poems are written in a special verse-form which Crabbe seems to have used when writing about disordered states of mind and the hallucinogenic effects of opium, to which he was addicted.

The notebook belonged to my great-great-great-great-aunt, Sarah Hoare, who was probably Crabbe's most intimate friend in his later years. Her papers have otherwise nearly all disappeared, a loss for which her friend William Wordsworth is partly to blame.

The reason why *The Voluntary Insane* was left unpublished is not difficult to guess at. At the time it was written it would have been considered profoundly shocking: the more so as, distorted by nightmare, it draws on the central tragedy of Crabbe's own life.

The Discovery

For the past twenty years or so I have earned my living by discovering manuscripts; so when the notebook containing *The Voluntary Insane* turned up I was not unduly excited. There was one small, if unusual, detail about the discovery, though. I did not come across it in the course of business. It came to light among my own family papers.

The phrase 'family papers' perhaps exaggerates matters a little. In our case they barely covered the bottom of a small tin trunk. This was kept in my father's dressing-room (the name given to a small walk-in cupboard), next to several generations of shoes, one or two dusty hat-boxes (with LNER delivery labels still in place) and sundry old picture frames (chipped).

Among the contents of the trunk was a journal of a tour of the Continent inscribed by its author 'Marlborough Pryor—Hampstead', a typical enough example of the genre, from which I quote the opening (if only people had kept diaries when staying at home instead!):

> July 26 1827—
> At eleven o'clock in the morning I came on board the steam boat, had a delightful sail down the Thames, was much struck with Greenwich Hospital & down at Gravesend by the immense width of the River . . .

With this was a grant of the Freedom of the Borough of Banff conferred on his brother, Robert Pryor, my great-great-grandfather, dating from the same period, as well as an album of verse extracts, including 'The Burial of Sir John Moore at Coruña', 'The Peri's Song' from *Lalla Rookh*, verses by Bishop Heber and other popular gems of the period, inscribed 'Ellen Pryor Hampstead August 1827'; together with a few other bits and pieces.

Robert, Marlborough and Ellen were children of Thomas Marlborough Pryor, my great-great-great-grandfather; the name 'Marlborough' has been perpetuated in the family—my father's name being Robert Matthew Marlborough Pryor and mine Thomas Felix

Miniature of Thomas Marlborough Pryor,
Sarah Hoare's brother-in-law,
by George Engleheart

INTRODUCTION

Marlborough Pryor—not because of any ducal link with the Churchills but because Thomas Marlborough Pryor's mother, Martha, was the daughter of a Mr Thomas Marlborough. It was through her that the family inherited a string of profitable pubs in Hertfordshire (a deed listing them came up for auction not long ago). Had she been called anything else, I suspect the name would not have been taken up by the family with such enthusiasm.

My father fished the notebook out of his briefcase one day—7 December 1989, to be precise—after the Annual General Meeting, held at Hitchin, Hertfordshire, of Henry Kendall & Sons Limited, a family firm, now defunct, which in balmier days had operated from the City of London importing sugar and other commodities from Peru.

Unlike its companions in the trunk, the notebook bore no identifying inscription. What prompted my father to pop it into his briefcase and bring it along to the AGM was the fact that someone had taken a pair of scissors to it and removed a section, writing alongside 'cut out for the autograph'. My father, who had served in wartime intelligence, identifying German rocket launch-pads for the RAF to bomb and monitoring Enigma intercepts, but who had received no formal literary training, quite reasonably supposed that if someone thought it worthwhile cutting little bits out 'for the autograph', then the notebook had been written by someone whose writing was worth cutting out.

At the time of the discovery I was fresh from a ten-year stint flogging manuscripts for one of the London auction houses. It was my duty to catalogue several sales a year, and each sale would generally contain one or two fairly major discoveries, perhaps the most dramatic of these being a scrumpled bit of waste paper that turned out to be part of a lost play by John Webster, author of *The Duchess of Malfi*, and the only 'foul paper', or working draft, surviving from Shakespeare's time. Another discovery, also a pocket-sized notebook and dating from the same year as ours, was the original of Hazlitt's *Liber Amoris*, that account of an erotic obsession that so shocked his contemporaries, which even Hazlitt's grandson, preparing a new edition in 1894, had written off as probably destroyed. The little volume in Hazlitt's handwriting arrived unannounced one day in the morning post. With it was a covering letter enquiring whether it was worth selling. The same post brought a signed photograph of Adolf Hitler belonging to a prison guard in Northern Ireland, which we declined to sell, and a typed letter by Robert Baden Powell, founder of the Boy Scouts, which we did not think worth enough to sell.

Suffering from discovery fatigue, I had left the auction house early in 1986, exchanging my company car for a company bicycle. Ever since, I have worked, as the blurb to *The Faber Book of Letters* which I edited at about this time puts it, 'with archive material and manuscripts in a freelance consultative capacity' (my job is not always easy to describe). In practice, this has meant that I have found myself working on and off for all the London auction houses, and having more undiscovered manuscripts thrust upon me than ever. When I discover *Love's Labour Won* I shall retire.

This, then, was why my father passed the notebook on to me. It was obvious from the first glance that it consisted of poetry, and that, from all the scribblings and crossings-out, it was not just a copy. This was enough to make my archival nostrils twitch.

Crabbe was my first guess. I was vaguely aware that there had existed some sort of link between him and my family. There was, I knew, a snuff-box at home engraved with a presentation inscription on the lid from him to some multiple great-aunt or other; there was also in the library, a room with one low bookcase with a broken marble top, dropped by a pre-war housemaid, a set of his *Poems* with a bit torn from one of his original letters glued into the first volume. The handwriting of the notebook seemed to correspond with what I could remember of Crabbe's, although this, the crucial point at issue, needed checking.

I took the notebook back with me to London that evening and was able to compare it with examples of Crabbe's handwriting illustrated in standard reference works. My first guess had been right. The handwriting of the notebook was his; and as the volume consisted of poetry, rather than laundry lists or sermons, the discovery was of some consequence. But the chances were that the poetry was either published or, if unpublished, so minor as to be not worth publishing except as an academic exercise. Over the next few days I dipped and browsed, and one stanza particularly struck me. This was one of the sections that had been 'cut out for the autograph' with the removed passage copied in pencil on the facing page:

> Love makes his way through many Tears;
>   He hates although he courts repose:
> His food is Danger, Terror, Fears;
>   Consent and Kindness are his Foes.
>   If he has nothing to oppose
> His restless spirit, he retreats;
>   Debates awhile; then off he goes,
> And loves the very frown he meets.

This belonged to a poem called 'The Irish Lovers'. As far as I could work out—there was so much crossing-out and jumping to and fro from stanza to stanza that I could not be certain—the notebook contained four long poems, 'Sir Denys Banger', 'The Voluntary Insane', 'The Irish Lovers' and 'The Madman's Dream'. The other detail I noticed at this stage was that 'The Madman's Dream' had a wonderful—wonderfully bad, that is—opening:

> There was a Seat at Linford in the Vale,
> A large old Building, advertised for Sale . . .

First stop, as always, was the London Library. There I found a three-volume edition of Crabbe's *Complete Poetical Works* that the Oxford University Press had brought out the year before (stamped as having arrived in the library on 17 August 1988). From this fresh-minted and impeccably sourced edition I learned that three of the four poems in the notebook were unknown and unpublished, except for some scattered stanzas tying in with 'The Voluntary Insane', and that the fourth, 'The Madman's Dream', existed in a shorter version called 'The Insanity of Ambitious Love'.

At this point I should perhaps apologise to the Oxford editors for not having discovered the notebook earlier. The timing, though, could have been even worse. When Hazlitt's *Liber Amoris* landed on my desk, a scholarly edition, written without benefit of the original, was actually in the process of being printed, and was thus (in some respects at least) obsolete before it was published. It is generally acknowledged in the bookselling world that major discoveries have a habit of happening only after the relevant collected edition has appeared.

I should also add that had some sixth sense prompted the Oxford editors to ask my family whether we owned anything by Crabbe I would have searched the library, something I had done often before, and told them that no, we didn't have any family papers. Until that AGM I did not know of the existence of the trunk in the dressing-room.

With the Oxford edition already published, there was no great hurry. The stable had already been vacated. I used the notebook as an excuse for paying a visit on the late Jock Murray, whose firm in Albemarle Street had been Crabbe's last publisher. He kindly showed me some very similar Crabbe compositional notebooks that the firm had in their archives. Apart from that I did nothing about it for a couple of years, devoting myself instead to a study of the 'little eyases' in *Hamlet* which I spun into a book called *The Mirror and the Globe*.

Having got the 'little eyases' out of the way, I commissioned an out-of-work auction-house colleague, now a distinguished curator, to prepare an initial transcript of the notebook. This was duly done, and another year or so went by. Then one day, 2 March 1993, I sat down at my word-processor with the notebook at my side to knock the preliminary transcript into shape. The poem I started with (it seemed the least complicated to unravel) was *The Voluntary Insane*.

And then came the moment in the whole long-drawn-out saga that, for me, stands out. This was when I realised that the notebook was special, that it was something out of the ordinary; when I realised that I had a true work of art on my hands.

The treasure had been lying under my nose all the while. I do not know when the tin trunk had been deposited in the dressing-room, but it had probably been within my reach nearly all my adult life. So this particular Great Discovery represents less a case of the intrepid adventurer setting forth and attaining his goal than that of the inattentive and elusive waiter whose eye has at long last been caught by a famished diner.

Externals of a Life

Further discoveries remained to be made. They came about not from studying the manuscript itself but from digging into the text of the poem, while at the same time exploring both Crabbe's early life—a life lived in a world that now seems almost unbearably remote—and the world of his dreams; two submerged entities that between them produced the ambergris that is *The Voluntary Insane.* But first it may be helpful to give a brief outline of the externals of Crabbe's life, bearing in mind that many people know of him only as the author of the tale upon which Benjamin Britten based his opera *Peter Grimes.*

The chief authority for information on Crabbe's biography is the *Life* published by his elder son George in 1834, two years after his death. The son tells us that most of this was written while his father was still alive, and certainly in the account given of his father's childhood and youth, which must have been furnished directly by him, we are made aware of a voice talking out of a long-vanished world. These word-pictures are extraordinarily vivid. All subsequent biographies have been dependent on the younger George's *Life*, the most thorough to date being René Huchon's *George Crabbe and his Times*, first published in 1907 and reissued in 1968.

George Crabbe the poet was born on Christmas Eve 1752 at Aldborough, the small fishing town on the Suffolk coast which Benjamin Britten was afterwards to make famous. The spelling has since been altered to the equally unphonetic Aldeburgh; but faithful to the usage of Crabbe's time, and not wishing to emend my own name to Marleburgh, I have here retained the old spelling.

Crabbe's family was, in René Huchon's pungent phrase, 'too obscure to have a history'. His father, also called George, was a collector of salt-duties at the town. The son was educated locally then apprenticed to an apothecary. He met his future wife Sarah Elmy in 1772, and at about this time had his first poems, in which he celebrated his love of 'Mira', as he called her, published in local ladies' magazines. Having completed his apprenticeship in 1775, he set up as an apothecary and surgeon to the poor at Aldborough. That year his first separately-published poem, *Inebriety*, was published anonymously (the title being perhaps indicative of future preoccupations).

He then tried to establish himself in London, bringing out a further poem, *The Candidate*, in 1780. When his fortunes were at their lowest ebb he made a desperate appeal to Edmund Burke, which met with a generous and justly celebrated response. Burke helped him publish a third poem, *The Library*, in 1781. He also encouraged him to take orders and secured him the patronage of the Duke of Rutland, whose domestic chaplain he became. Crabbe afterwards held a living at Muston in Leicestershire (although living for much of the time in Suffolk), and in 1814 was appointed Rector of Trowbridge in Wiltshire, where he remained for the rest of his life.

The pinnacle of his early career as a poet was achieved with the publication, under his own name for the first time, of *The Village* in 1783, which Dr Johnson described as 'original, vigorous, and elegant' and to which he and Burke contributed a few finishing touches. At the end of that year Crabbe was able to marry Sarah Elmy. In 1785 he brought out a satirical poem, *The Newspaper*, which proved less successful than its predecessor. Perhaps discouraged by this, he published no more poems for the next twenty-two years.

His long silence was broken in 1807 with the publication of *Poems*, which besides old work contained the first of the verse-tales that were to establish his reputation the second time round, and for which he is now generally remembered. The *Poems* of 1807 were succeeded by three volumes which made him one of the most successful poets of the Regency period: *The Borough* of 1810, which included 'Peter Grimes' and 'Ellen Orford', the *Tales* of 1812, and the *Tales from the Hall* of 1819. A collected edition of his poems, together with a volume of *Posthumous Tales* and his son George's biography, was published in 1834, two years after his death.

Crabbe had six children, only two of whom, George and John Waldron, survived into adulthood, both following him into the church. After the death of his wife in 1813, he formed a number of attachments to younger women. The most important of these was his friendship with Sarah Hoare, daughter of Samuel Hoare, a Quaker banker, who lived at Heath House, Hampstead. Her mother having died in 1783, her father had in 1788 married Hannah Sterry, who was only a few years older than she. After Samuel's death in 1825, Sarah and Hannah continued to live together and assumed the role of literary mentors, keepers of the sacred flame, to whom Crabbe submitted all his compositions. It was to Hannah that he gave the snuff-box that I could remember from home.

At the Hoares', Crabbe was introduced to William Wilberforce, Joanna Baillie, Maria Edgeworth and Mrs Siddons, and while staying at Heath House he would take rambles with Wordsworth on Hampstead Heath. He visited them once a year from 1817 till 1830, sometimes staying for weeks at a time, and would also join them on excursions to their old family property, Cliff House, at Cromer, Norfolk, and other resorts. In the last weeks of his life he visited Clifton with them, where he witnessed the Bristol Riots. He died, aged seventy-nine, at Trowbridge Rectory on 3 February 1832.

Sarah Hoare died unmarried in 1856, in the same year as her stepmother; but she had a sister, also called Hannah, and it was this sister who brings my family into the story. She married Thomas Marlborough Pryor, and so was mother of Marlborough, Robert and Ellen Pryor, respectively Continental diarist, Freeman of the Borough of Banff and verse anthologist, denizens of the tin trunk, where they were to languish over the years in company with an anonymous notebook from which some leaves had been 'cut out for the autograph'.

Opium and the Augustan Imagination

For most of his adult life, George Crabbe was addicted to opium. He was first prescribed the drug in about 1789 after suffering a dizzy spell and collapsing in the street at Ipswich. His son George describes this episode in his *Life*:

> the late Dr. Club was sent for, who, after a little examination, saw through the case with great judgment. 'There is nothing the matter with your head,' he observed, 'nor any apoplectic tendency; let the digestive organs bear the whole blame: you must take opiates.' From that time his health began to amend rapidly, and his constitution was renovated; a rare effect of opium, for that drug

Watercolour of Sarah Hoare by Josiah Slater

almost always inflicts some partial injury, even when it is necessary: but to him it was only salutary—and to a constant but slightly increasing dose of it may be attributed his long and generally healthy life.

But unlike Coleridge, with Crabbe this has never been much of a selling point.

There is however a group of Crabbe poems which do relate to his addiction, and were clearly written under the influence of, or at least describe, his opium trances. One of these, 'Sir Eustace Grey', was published in the first of the volumes to appear after his twenty-two-year silence, the *Poems* of 1807, and was greatly admired. Another, 'The World of Dreams', appeared in the *Posthumous Tales* published in 1834. Most of the rest remained unpublished until Arthur Pollard brought out his *New Poems by George Crabbe* in 1960. Further additions were made to the canon by Norma Dalrymple-Champneys and Arthur Pollard in their *Complete Poetical Works* of 1988 (the Oxford University Press edition already mentioned).

These dream poems, which Alethea Hayter has analysed in her classic study, *Opium and the Romantic Imagination*, 1968, are generally written in eight-line stanzas rhyming *ababbcbc*. The group as a whole is discussed by the Oxford editors in their general note on 'The influence of opium on Crabbe's verse'. All the poems in the newly discovered notebook (hereafter referred to as the Hoare Notebook) follow this dream poem format.

By contrast, nearly all those poems by which Crabbe is best known, including 'Ellen Orford' and 'Peter Grimes', are written in rhyming or 'heroic' couplets, the verse-form favoured throughout the eighteenth century. By the time he came to embark on his second

career, in the early nineteenth century, they were to
mark him out as belonging to the old school.

Throughout, as the Romantic Age came and went,
the poet whose verses Dr Johnson had once polished
stuck to his heroics. 'There is', Tennyson observed, 'a
tramp, tramp, tramp, a merciless sledge-hammer thud
about his lines which suits his subjects'.

While Crabbe's powers of observation were gener-
ally recognised, this meant that his verse was considered
rather old-fashioned, verging on the 'unpoetic', by the
younger generation of burgeoning Romantics. He was
famously described as 'Pope in worsted stockings' by
the brothers James and Horatio Smith in their *Rejected
Addresses* of 1812. Which is probably why Byron ad-
mired him so, calling him 'Nature's sternest Painter, yet
the best' (words which were to be engraved on his
memorial in Trowbridge Church); and why Jane
Austen, on hearing of his wife's death, told her sister
Cassandra that she was going to be the next Mrs Crabbe.

Hazlitt complained that he 'describes the interior of a
cottage like a person sent there to distrain for rent'; and
Coleridge grumbled that he had 'an absolute defect of
the high imagination'. The young Carlyle wrote of him
in 1816 that 'in addition to great powers of correct
description, he possesses all the sagacity of an anatom-
ist in searching into the stormy passions of the human
heart—and all the apathy of an anatomist in describing
them'.

By the end of the nineteenth century, his work was
generally being considered as 'verse', albeit very good
verse, rather than 'poetry'. George Saintsbury said he
didn't have wings, and concluded: 'Crabbe was not a
poet. But I have not the least intention of denying that
he was great, and all but the greatest among English
writers.'

But there was still that small group of opium-inspired poems which were admired as being the exception to the rule. They were, as the others were not, 'lyrical'. They did have wings. But they weren't, quite, all there. They were not integrated into the main stream. They lacked the enduring qualities—those of the inspired anatomiser of the human heart—that distinguish his verse-tales.

In 1847, George Gillifan, a critic of the Spasmodic school, who admired those few opium-poems that were known to him, seemed to sense this when he remarked that 'We have repeatedly expressed our opinion, that in Crabbe there lay a higher power than he ever exerted'.

Rash though it may be, it is tempting to see Gillifan here making a prophecy which *The Voluntary Insane* fulfils. I think even Saintsbury would categorise this particular verse-tale as 'poetry' as well as 'great writing'. In it, it seems to me, the waking Crabbe makes use of the wings otherwise reserved for his dreams. It is a dramatic poem of lyrical impulse that delves deep into the human heart.

The Wife

The Voluntary Insane is a poem about a girl's madness after the death of a baby in her care. Crabbe's wife endured a similar fate. Four of her children died in infancy, causing her severe depression. After the death of a fifth, her six-year-old son William in 1796, she had a breakdown from which she never properly recovered. She suffered acute and debilitating depression until her own death seventeen years later, on 21 October 1813.

Crabbe's son wrote that 'during the hotter months of

almost every year, she was oppressed by the deepest dejection of spirits I ever witnessed in any one', but that there were 'long intervals' when, 'if her spirits were a little too high, the relief to herself and others was great indeed'.

Crabbe himself wrote to Alethea Brereton Lewis, a friend of theirs from early days, that his wife had remained in other ways perfectly sane until six months or so before her death, retaining the capacity for rational thought even when her mind was clouded by nervous depression.

Similarly, the Maiden of the poem is seen as being sane in every respect, apart from her intermittent bouts of profound melancholy and her haunting by the spectre of the infant. This is the conundrum around which the early part of the poem revolves.

The Uncle

In *The Voluntary Insane*, the Maiden has no father, but she has a rich uncle. The Uncle has an only child. When that child dies the Maiden becomes sole heir to the Uncle's fortune. In real life, Crabbe's wife had no father; he had, the son tells us, died 'some time before Mr. Crabbe knew the family'. But she did have a prosperous uncle. The uncle had an only child. When that child died Crabbe's wife became heir to her uncle's estate.

Crabbe's bride was called Sarah Elmy. Her family was better off than his. Her uncle, John—or Jack (his unmarried sister who lived with him called him Jacky)—Tovell, had an estate of about £800 per annum and, according to Crabbe's son, maintained an establishment that was 'that of the first-rate yeoman of the period—the Yeoman that already began to be styled by courtesy an Esquire'. Jack Tovell lived in a large house called Ducking Hall, in the village of Parham, some ten miles inland from Aldborough.

Jack Tovell's only child was a girl called Jane or 'Jenney', 'a fine hale girl of fourteen, humoured by her mother, adored by her father'. She died suddenly, 'cut off in a few days by an inflammatory sore throat'; snuffed out like the child in the poem, who has his frail life 'pressed' out of him: and although the poem does not specify which area of the baby's body was being pressed—it is something one shrinks from visualising—Crabbe presumably had in mind the baby's throat or thorax. Before taking holy orders, Crabbe had practised as a doctor; and the description of Jenney's death given in the son's biography must have come directly from him.

After Jenney's death, Crabbe and his wife became Jack Tovell's inheritors, his estate having been left in equal shares to his two sisters, one of whom was Sarah Crabbe's widowed mother. The Hall would become theirs, and Crabbe, the only male, would become its master. The uncle was fully aware of this, and of how this stranger had come into his beloved daughter's inheritance. He told him to his face. It was something Crabbe was never to forget. The incident forms one of the most vivid incidents in the son's *Life*:

> I have heard my father describe his astonishment at learning, as he rode into the stable-yard, that Miss Tovell was *dead*. It seemed as if it must be a fiction, so essential did her life appear to her parents. He said he never recollected to have felt any dread equal to that of entering the house on this occasion; for my mother might now be considered as, in part at least, Mr. Tovell's heir, and he anticipated the reception she should meet with, and well knew that he must suffer from the first bitterness of minds

too uncultivated to suppress their feelings. He found it as painful as he had foreboded. Mr. Tovell was seated in his arm-chair, in stern silence; but the tears coursed each other over his manly face. His wife was weeping violently, her head reclining on the table. One or two female friends were there, to offer consolation. After a long silence, Mr. Tovell observed,—'She is now out of *every body's* way, poor girl!' One of the females remarked, that it was wrong, very wrong, to grieve, because she was gone to a better place. 'How do I know where she is gone?' was the bitter reply; and then there was another long silence.

When Jack Tovell died, Crabbe and his family moved into Ducking Hall. They had now physically, as well as legally, supplanted the dead Jenney.

The Priest

In *The Voluntary Insane* the girl eventually tells her tale to a Priest and, through him, tells her story to us. The Priest acts as narrator. Crabbe, as writer of the poem, is of course its ultimate narrator. He was also an ordained priest of the Church of England, serving, at the time of writing, as Rector of Trowbridge in Wiltshire.

It was both as priest and husband that he watched at his wife's bedside. He afterwards wrote to their friend Alethea Brereton Lewis: 'I had long, very long to watch a Being whose Mind was growing cloudy & at last became nearly dark, yet with Coruscations & Strugglings for the Light at times.'

Like the Priest in the poem, he was a man of moderate views and humane sympathy, preaching repentance and forgiveness. In this he is in marked contrast to the ranting Preacher to whom the distressed

Maiden turns earlier in the poem. The Preacher is described as a 'harsh relentless Guide':

> Who planted Terror in her Breast:
>   Who to her Soul, the Peace denied
> That his elected Crew possessed.   (557–60)

Crabbe's ministry was disturbed by just such preachers. The most threatening, according to his son, were the Huntingtonians. These were followers of the eccentric coalheaver-turned-preacher William Huntington S.S. (standing for 'Sinner Saved').

The Huntingtonians should not be confused with the Huntingdonians, with a 'd', who were a more respectable group taking their name from the 'Lady Huntingdon's Connection', established by George Whitefield. This was the sect to which the poet William Cowper, through his spiritual mentor John Newton, was allied.

Although they drew their support from different social classes, both Huntingtonians and Huntingdonians preached a Calvinist doctrine of predestination. By this it was held that salvation was reserved for the elect. William Cowper, who like Mrs Crabbe suffered from appalling depressive illness, believed that he was not among those who had been chosen; that he was, in other words, damned.

Crabbe's son tells us that after one particularly long period of absence from his parish, his father had returned to find that the Methodists had been making inroads into his flock and, even worse, that a Huntingtonian had been 'spreading in the same neighbourhood the pernicious fanaticism of his half-crazy master'; and that one of his own servants, 'a conceited ploughman', had 'set up for a Huntingtonian preacher himself'. The son adds: 'I mention these things, because they may throw light on some passages in my father's later poetry' (for Crabbe's own account of the Priest-versus-Preacher divide, see the Preface and Letters III and IV of *The Borough*).

It is to the Priest, the good middle-of-the-road Church of England parson, rather than to the Preacher, that the Maiden tells her tale. He is told that she had many virtues; but all to no avail. Parson Crabbe knew that his wife, too, had many virtues. But all to no avail. The son tells us:

> so large a portion of her married life was clouded by her lamentable disorder, that I find written by my father on the outside of a beautiful letter of her own, dated long before this calamity, 'Nothing can be more sincere than this, nothing more reasonable and affectionate; and yet happiness was denied.'

So perhaps after all it is the Preacher who has the last word. Perhaps Crabbe (to paraphrase Blake), being a true poet, was of the Preacher's party without knowing it. Perhaps in some part of his soul he believed that grace had been withheld from his wife, and that she was, as Cowper thought he was, damned.

Certainly very few hymns measure up to the lines Crabbe gives the Maiden when she tells the Priest that grace has been denied her. It is as if one of Cowper's *Olney Hymns* had been turned inside out. As author of 'The Castaway', he would have recognised their terror:

> This Faith you teach, and this you Strive
> To force on all! as Children play
> From Hand to Hand to bear alive
> The idle fire that must decay;
> So you from Mind to Mind convey
> This Faith, and all to take agree:
> Not so—for I the forfeit pay.
> The trembling fire goes out with me.   (1177–84)

INTRODUCTION

The Nightmare: All was Misery and Degradation

Crabbe has left us an account of one of his nightmares in his London Journal for 21 July 1817. On first glance, it seems irritatingly vague, and by the standards of his fellow opium-eater De Quincey comparatively mundane:

> I was incommoded by dreams, such as would cure vanity for a time in any mind where they could gain admission . . . Awake, I had been with the high, the apparently happy: we were very pleasantly engaged, and my last thoughts were cheerful. Asleep, all was misery and degradation, not my own only, but of those who had been.— That horrible image of servility and baseness—that mercenary and commercial manner! It is the work of the imagination, I suppose; but it is very strange. I must leave it.

But the details that Crabbe gives us here—vague though they are—are in fact both significant and unexpectedly revealing.

He does not talk of dreams or nightmares, but of 'misery and degradation'. The phrase is thus made synonymous with nightmare. 'Misery' is also the working title he used when writing *The Voluntary Insane*. It appears at the head of a very early draft of some stanzas preserved in one of the Murray notebooks (discussed below), and appears underneath the title in our manuscript, which reads in full:

> The voluntary-Insane.
> Misery.—
> Part 1st—
> The Character. before.

So the link between poem and nightmare is a very concrete one. They share the same name.

Crabbe specifies that it was not just he who was

subjected to 'misery and degradation', but also 'those who had been'. Here he is referring to his dead wife, the wife who had gone mad; possibly also his dead children, the children whose deaths had driven her mad; possibly also the dead Jenney, the heiress whom he and his wife had supplanted; and possibly, too, his wife's dead uncle, old Jack Tovell of Ducking Hall.

Terence Bareham, writing of course without benefit of having seen *The Voluntary Insane*, suggests that the 'mercenary and commercial manner' of this nightmare might reflect Crabbe's uncertain position with regard to his wife's family and their greater wealth; and adds that 'the relationship with his wife's family yields poetic capital time and again'. *The Voluntary Insane—* itself a species of 'misery'—turns this relationship into nightmare. In it, the Maiden kills the baby so that she can secure its inheritance. She murders a child for money. Her 'mercenary and commercial manner' lies at the heart of the tragedy.

Dream Landscapes: the Moated Hall

It is of course not suggested that the Maiden is a 'portrait' of Mrs Crabbe, or the Priest of Crabbe, or the Preacher of the Huntingtonian-Ploughman, or the Uncle of Jack Tovell, or the baby of Crabbe's own child; although surely only someone who had seen a baby close to, and knew from their own experience that it had not yet secured its passage into the world, could have come up with the extraordinary Sylvia-Plath-exact image of

> The half unsealed and cloudy Eye,
> That shut again; for Life was new,
> Not perfect Life . . .   (1011–13)

They may not be portraits, but they are where Crabbe's fictional people and landscapes are rooted; and, as Terence Bareham observes, Crabbe's fictive roots do seem to tap more deeply into his wife's family than anywhere else.

Take, for example, Ducking Hall. This was an old-world, atmospheric house. Crabbe's son, who later lived there himself, describes it as being large with a 'surrounding moat' and 'rookery'. In *The Voluntary Insane*, the Maiden is described wandering:

> Unseen by Day, she roams by Night,
>   Or by the Cliff that bounds the Sea,
> Or by the melancholy Light
>   Of Elms, where Rooks returning flee;
>   Or round the reedy Moat where she
> Watches with fixed and troubled Look . . . (129–34)

The picture is not precisely that of Ducking Hall, which, being ten miles inland, was not by the sea; but rather contains elements—the moat, rookery, melancholy elm-light—of Ducking Hall. It is a composite landscape, as most dream landscapes are; a capriccio of early-remembered features.

The cliff may recall the cliff above Aldborough, where, the son tells us, Crabbe himself used to wander brooding and where one day, while gazing into a leech pond (a habit the Maiden seems to have picked up from him), he 'determined to go to London and venture all'.

Or, more probably, since we are told the cliff 'bounds' the sea, it may recall Lake Lothing, a natural basin worn by the sea eight miles east of Beccles, near 'a sweet little villa called Normanston', where 'four or five spinsters of independent fortune had formed a sort of Protestant nunnery', and where Sarah Elmy stayed during part of her courtship by Crabbe, having her education polished by these good ladies as a preliminary to her entry into society.

Dream characters, like dream landscapes, have their composite element. For example, when we are first introduced to the Uncle in *The Voluntary Insane*, he is described as being 'A Man grave, prudent, thoughtful, still' (806). Attributes which are conventional enough, but fitting for the role assigned to him, that of a rich merchant.

So it comes as something of a surprise when, later on in the story, he is pictured celebrating his child's recovery by rushing off to the pub:

> My Uncle's Folly sought the Inn—
>   To talk of his recovered Boy
>   And drench the Clowns in drunken Joy . . . (939–41)

Which is neither grave, nor prudent, nor thoughtful, nor still.

But the character is in fact merely reverting to type. For Crabbe's son records how 'on ordinary days' at Ducking Hall

> as if by instinct some old acquaintance would glide in for the evening's carousal, and then another, and another. If four or five arrived, the punchbowl was taken down, and emptied and filled again.

As a result of which, we are told, Jack Tovell 'seldom went to bed sober'.

Dream Landscapes: the Ship and the Cliff

The Voluntary Insane is by no means unique among Crabbe's poems in drawing on these youthful memories. For example in the *Tales of the Hall*, written only a few years before *The Voluntary Insane* and published in

1819, he employs an autobiographical framework within which the tales are set.

The stories are told by two brothers, David and Richard. Richard, the younger of the two, courts and marries a maid called Matilda. According to Crabbe's later biographer, René Huchon, this particular Matilda—the name does crop up elsewhere in Crabbe's tales—draws many of her features from his real-life bride; while Richard and his brother are both self-portraits, bearing 'more or less striking resemblances to the author'. The childhood of Richard is almost identical with what is known of Crabbe's own.

At the beginning of *The Voluntary Insane*, after a brief narratorial flourish, the same name is also trundled forward. The Maiden is introduced to us as 'Matilda' (33). The narrator then goes on to adumbrate her virtues. This is the only time she is referred to by name.

In the dream landscape of *The Voluntary Insane* we are shown the moat and rookery of Ducking Hall; but there is also the cliff upon which the Maiden wanders and the sea, possibly drawn from memories of the cliff at Aldborough, or from memories of Lake Lothing with its spinster community.

The cliff crops up again in some well-known lines from the 'Adventures of Richard Concluded' in the *Tales of the Hall*. Here the setting definitely does seem to be that of the Beccles coast around Lake Lothing, with Crabbe travelling to visit his bride-to-be in her nunnery. His *alter ego*, Richard, tells us of a happy summons:

> Such days have been—a day of days was one
> When, rising gaily with the rising sun,
> I took my way to join a happy few,
> Known not to me, but whom Matilda knew,
> To whom she went a guest, and message sent,
> 'Come thou to us,' and as a guest I went.

There are two ways to Brandon—by the heath
Above the cliff, or on the sand beneath,
Where the small pebbles, wetted by the wave,
To the new day reflected lustre gave:
At first above the rocks I made my way,
Delighted looking at the spacious bay,
And the large fleet that to the northward steer'd
Full sail, that glorious in my view appear'd . . . (170–83)

The Voluntary Insane gives us an almost identical land-
scape, although refracted through an altered lens; a
contrasted panel from the same diptych. The image is
no longer one of sparkling promise—of a large fleet
under full sail—but of absence; and has something of
the haunting quality of a painting by Crabbe's German
contemporary, Caspar David Friedrich. This time it is
the Priest who is Crabbe's *alter ego*. He tells us of
Matilda's withdrawal from life:

Days, Months and Seasons passed Away,
    And nothing I beheld or heard;
I missed her in her Haunts by day,
    By night no longer she appeared:
    By our tall Cliff the Coaster steered,
Her Voyage unmarked by us on shore . . .   (697–702)

The 'Misery' Verses

A very early draft for a section of *The Voluntary Insane* is
to be found in one of the notebooks held in the archives
of Crabbe's last publishers, John Murray. It was first
published in 1988 under the title 'Misery' in the Oxford
edition of the *Complete Poetical Works*. The Oxford
editors describe it as 'a rough, partly illegible, and much
corrected draft'.

The Oxford editors note that its heading, 'Misery',
'may not have been intended as a title—Crabbe some-

times used headings in his notebooks suggesting what was to follow'. In the Hoare Notebook, the word 'Misery' appears underneath the main title. As we have seen, this was a word Crabbe associated with his nightmares.

It clearly represents a very early draft for *The Voluntary Insane*, from which the only element of the plot discernible is that the haunted Maiden is suffering from melancholia following the death of the child; but there is no hint of her terrible secret (for further details see Appendix III).

It seems probable that, at this early stage, Crabbe was still groping towards the overall shape that the poem was to take. And it is the overall layering of the finished poem into its different narrative voices— exemplified by the Websterian horror of the Maiden's 'O! Why so drop my hand?' (1016) or the pastoral idiom of the last stanza whereby the Maiden's death is shored to silence—that is so brilliantly managed in *The Voluntary Insane*, and which makes it so much more than merely a longish stretch of verse with a few good bits to quote from.

Apart from the fact that the draft and the finished poem are both headed with the working title 'Misery', there are three other features—two within, one without—that tie the 'Misery' draft to the final version.

The first stanza of the 'Misery' draft, beginning 'She read of Scenes where Horror dwells', is marked 'Stanza 7'. In the final version, this stanza is marked in pencil as being number 7 (although ultimately it is pushed back one place by the insertion of an extra stanza between numbers 1 and 2, and in the printed text stands as number 8). So the annotation on the 'Misery' manuscript refers either to the Hoare Notebook, or to an intermediate text similar at this point.

Above the final stanza of the 'Misery' draft Crabbe has written in his formal hand (used mainly for writing titles and headings): 'Priest and Friend. P. You cannot then believe the Tale/ Nor your contemptuous Thoughts disguise'. This is the place where the final manuscript begins (the first of the narrative voices); although the Priest/ Friend stage-direction, a rather clumsy narrative device typical of Crabbe's late verse-tales, has mercifully been dropped.

The external link is provided by the cover of the notebook in which the 'Misery' draft is found. This is inscribed with a list of contents, among which is included: 'Misery verse. Copied for Miss Hoare 1824. March 1822'.

The straight-forward interpretation of this would be that Crabbe wrote the 'Misery' verses in March 1822, and copied them out for Sarah Hoare in 1824, long after the final poem had been completed. This, I think, is still the most likely interpretation, although it does imply an interest on Sarah Hoare's part which is more typical of modern academia than of her own time: when, eighty years later, A.W. Ward was editing Crabbe's poems for the Cambridge University Press, he was given the opportunity of examining the manuscript of *The Library*, but declined the offer as being of no interest.

The other interpretation that could be placed on the inscription is that the 'Misery' verses were drafted in March 1822, and then expanded into the final version—which stretches the meaning of 'Copied' rather—in 1824, and then given to Sarah Hoare. However, this clashes with other evidence which suggests a date for the finished poem of 1822, rather than 1824 (see the section on dating below).

In whatever way the 'Misery' verses were copied, the

inscription does establish that Sarah Hoare was involved with the actual composition of the poem, and that this involvement ran beyond the mere ownership of the completed manuscript.

Crabbe is known to have discussed his poems with her and her stepmother, and gives a droll account of one of these sessions in a letter to his son George:

> To-morrow I have a kind of School—or say College Examination to undergo, in reading to M^{rs} and Miss Hoare, who are by no Means very easy to be satisfied and who would not easily permit me to do anything hastily or to undo what has been done.

One imagines that it was at just such a session that *The Voluntary Insane* was discussed.

Other Poems in the Hoare Notebook

There are three other poems in the Hoare Notebook, details of which are given in Appendix IV. They are: 'Sir Denys Banger', an extremely long (Crabbe's longest) and, it must be said, bad verse-tale, partly written in imitation of Byron's *Don Juan* (Byron in worsted stockings); 'The Irish Lovers', a verse-tale describing thwarted love; and 'The Madman's Dream', a longer reworking of the opium-dream poem first published in 1960 as 'The Insanity of Ambitious Love'. 'The Voluntary Insane' is the second poem in the Hoare Notebook, coming between 'Sir Denys Banger' and 'The Irish Lovers'.

The Physical Notebook

W.B. Yeats used to hum as he composed. Crabbe waved his hand up and down and collected plants:

While searching for and examining plants or insects, he was moulding verses into measure and smoothness. No one who observed him at these times could doubt that he enjoyed exquisite pleasure in composing. He had a degree of action while thus walking and versifying, which I hardly ever observed when he was preaching or reading. The hand was moved up and down; the pace quickened. He was, nevertheless, fond of considering poetical composition as a species of task and labour, and would say, 'I have been hard at work, and have had a good morning.'

The Hoare Notebook has a dozen or so dried plants pressed between its leaves, including several grasses (of which his son remarks: 'In botany, grasses, the most useful, but the least ornamental, were his favourites').

The notebook, which is of convenient size to fit into the pocket, is bound in half black calf with mottled brown papered boards (measuring 7½ × 5¾ ins, 9 × 2.5 cm). It was presumably bought at a stationer's. The book itself consists of 136 leaves (some mutilated). Inserted at the end is a stitched gathering of 12 leaves (the first mutilated) containing the conclusion of 'The Madman's Dream' (beginning at 'Away with fear and go with me . . .'). The paper of the notebook proper is watermarked 'Dusautoy & C°/ 1815'. The loosely inserted fascicle is watermarked 'Bath/ 1815'.

Written on the fly-leaf, in a special cypher that Crabbe was in the habit of using, is the memorandum (or injunction): 'M[?iss] HOARE'S + BETTER'; with another word in cypher (apparently: 'xxx TRAM—') written beneath the name of the giant-killer 'Tom Hickerthrift' (who receives a mention in Crabbe's 'Silford Hall', line 101) on the last leaf. Also on the fly-leaf is an extract in Crabbe's handwriting from a letter dated August 1819 which may, or may not, refer to the social inadequacies of William Wordsworth (see Appendix VI).

In general terms the Hoare Notebook is similar to other Crabbe notebooks that have survived. Crabbe's son records that his father left at his death twenty-one such notebooks. Of those that have been traced, most are now in the Murray archive or at the University Library, Cambridge. A full list and history of their dispersal is given in the Oxford *Complete Poetical Works* and the *Index of English Literary Manuscripts*. The Hoare Notebook, having been in my father's dressing-room at the time, is not recorded on either list.

The poems in the Hoare Notebook seem to have started life as fair copies. Then, either as he was writing out the poems or, in the case of the Byronic sections added to 'Sir Denys Banger', after he had finished writing them out, Crabbe would enter additions and revisions on the left-hand pages which had been left blank for the purpose. Sometimes, as stanzas are crossed out and bits added, the manuscript becomes quite complicated, with small pointing hands drawn against the text and instructions telling one where to jump next.

The manuscript of *The Voluntary Insane* itself is, then, essentially a fair copy and probably comes close to Crabbe's final intentions; although indubitably, had it been prepared for the press, further revisions would have been made.

One other feature of the Hoare Notebook is the fact that my great-great-great-great-aunt was, as we have seen, in the habit of snipping bits out of it (usually one or two eight-line stanzas at a time) and giving them away to autograph-collectors. This was fairly typical of the age. It is on record, for example, that Charles

Cowden Clarke snipped a Keats sonnet into thirteen sections and gave them away (which at little over a line a time shows less generosity).

Fortunately in most instances my aunt has written 'cut out for autograph', 'copied' or 'torn out' on the facing page, and transcribed the missing lines beneath. Her handwriting (which could have been clearer) can be checked against two autograph letters by her in the British Library among the Christopher Wordsworth papers, where there are also letters by her stepmother and niece, Ellen (Add. MSS., 46137, f.226 and 46138, f.135). A few other sections have been cut out and the missing part written out in what looks like a slightly later hand, which I have been unable to identify.

I had assumed when first preparing the transcript of the notebook's contents that Sarah Hoare had written out everything that her generous spirit had prompted her to remove. But this, unfortunately, is not the case. I have since discovered that a whole leaf had been sliced out by her, without the contents being transcribed, and given to her friend the Hampstead playwright Joanna Baillie. This is now at the Royal College of Surgeons (see Appendix V)—a fate of which Jung would have approved. This leaf was part of the opening of 'Sir Denys Banger' and would not have represented a great loss to literature.

A more serious problem concerns the end of the first section of *The Voluntary Insane* itself (line 120), where it might be thought that the sense is left hanging in mid-air. At this point a large part of a leaf has been cut out. The loss is not certain, as the few lines that remain have the appearance of having been crossed out. But there is the possibility of a stanza or two having gone missing here. Nor am I certain of my transcription of the manuscript at this point, so I may have added to the muddle.

The Date

The most immediate clue to the dating of *The Voluntary Insane* is held by the contents list of the Murray notebook in which the very early draft is to be found: 'Misery verse. Copied for Miss Hoare 1824. March 1822'. This I have already discussed. There are entries in the Murray notebook in the pages following on from the verses which are dated 22 March and 20 November 1821.

It appears that, while drafting the 'Misery' verses, Crabbe intended to use them as part of another poem called 'Joseph and Jesse', and there are links in subject matter between the two. A deleted stanza in *The Voluntary Insane* itself shows that Crabbe for a while wanted to link the completed tale to 'Joseph and Jesse' also, and then thought better of it. The Oxford editors are of the opinion that 'Joseph and Jesse' was 'probably written in 1822'. For a further discussion of the relationship between the two poems, see Appendix III, where the deleted stanza from *The Voluntary Insane* is printed.

The other poems in the Hoare Notebook provide further clues. 'The Madman's Dream' is not much help, though, in this regard. The original version of the poem, 'The Insanity of Ambitious Love' is dated November 1816. Both the original version and 'The Madman's Dream' contain allusions which suggest that Crabbe had at some point intended to include them in *Tales of the Hall* (1819). So all one can say about 'The Madman's Dream' is that it had been lying about in Crabbe's workshop for some time.

The first poem in the notebook, 'Sir Denys Banger',

provides more positive evidence. Like the 'Misery' verses and 'The Voluntary Insane', it appears to have links with the 'Joseph and Jesse' poem of 1822. In it Sir Denys's unfortunate elder brother is described as being 'fair/ As Jesse's son'. This gives one a prima face case for dating 'Sir Denys Banger' to about 1822.

But the most important clue afforded by 'Sir Denys Banger' lies in the *ottava-rima* stanzas written in imitation of Lord Byron's *Don Juan* (see Appendix IV). These have been entered into left-hand pages of the notebook (which Crabbe usually left blank in readiness for additional material), and were added after the main body of the poem had already been copied onto the facing right-hand pages. They must post-date 1818, the year when Byron published *Beppo*, his first exercise in *ottava-rima*; and they are likely to have been written after the summer of 1819, which saw the publication and *succès de scandale* of the first two Cantos of *Don Juan*, his masterpiece in the genre.

Crabbe's *ottava-rima* stanzas describe how Sir Denys, who 'much resembled One/ Childe Harold', flies 'pursued by Hate and Curses,/ To Greece'. It is hard to believe that this does not refer to Byron's famous expedition to Greece, made in the summer of 1823. By the same token, it seems extremely unlikely that Crabbe would have written his spoof, which is highly critical of Byron's abuse of his poetic skills, after 14 May 1824, the day when news of Byron's death reached England. Bad taste apart, there would not have been much point.

The physical layout of the Hoare Notebook shows that the *ottava-rima* stanzas postdate 'The Voluntary Insane', the next poem in the book, as well as 'Sir Denys Banger'. By the time Crabbe came to add the thirty-six Byronic stanzas he had not left himself much space, and a terrible confusion ensues, with little hands pointing this way and that. Had the pages running on from 'Sir Denys Banger' been still left blank he could have used these instead and saved himself, not to say his modern transcriber, a good deal of trouble. It seems reasonable therefore to conclude that 'The Voluntary Insane', as well as 'Sir Denys Banger', had already been entered into the notebook when Crabbe decided to add the thirty-six stanzas. As the latter probably date from the second half of 1823 or early 1824, the rest could well have been written in 1822 or early 1823.

Apart from the contents list on the cover of the Murray notebook, there are two other pieces of external evidence which may help pin down the date of *The Voluntary Insane*. These are references by Crabbe to his unpublished writings in his correspondence with the Quaker author Mary Leadbeater, now held in the British Library (Egerton MS 3709a).

The first reference can probably be discounted. In a letter of 30 October 1817, Crabbe tells Mrs Leadbeater that he has by him 'some few things in the Manner of Sir Eustace Grey'. It seems more likely that he is here referring to poems such as 'The Madman's Dream' (or its earlier emanation 'The Insanity of Ambitious Love') and 'The World of Dreams', which are indeed written in the manner of 'Sir Eustace Grey', than he is to *The Voluntary Insane*, which shares the stanza-pattern of 'Sir Eustace Grey', but not its manner.

The second reference is in a letter of 25 November 1822. Here Crabbe tells Mrs Leadbeater that he has 'some not-perfectly-formed Intention of publishing three or four Pieces of Versification'. One of these pieces is an oriental tale by Henry Gally Knight, which Crabbe has versified. To this he intends to add:

two or three other Attempts; One more Essay at the
Description of a kind of Insanity or Hallucination!—with
these are some Trifles which certain Friends—M^rs &
Miss Hoare, the Wife & unmarried Daughter of Saml
Hoare the Banker in Lombard Street—whom I have
known & loved—for it is nearly the same thing—some
four or five Years—which these Ladies permit me to
think of publishing & they are so jealous of my Credit
that what they permit, I may allow myself has something
of the Vis poetica in it.

Taking all the other strands of evidence into account, it
seems to me highly likely that this 'One more Essay at
the Description of a kind of Insanity or Hallucination'
does indeed refer to *The Voluntary Insane.*

If this is so, it would mean that *The Voluntary Insane*
had been begun by March 1822, the date of the 'Misery'
verses, and was more or less finished by 25 November
1822.

A Visit to Sir Walter Scott

The Voluntary Insane apart, 1822 was a significant year
for Crabbe. That August he went up to Edinburgh to
stay with his ardent admirer, Sir Walter Scott (who was
later to pay him the unsurpassed tribute of having only
Crabbe and the Bible read to him during his last
illness).

Crabbe's jaunt to Edinburgh coincided with the
celebrated visit of the tartan-trewed George IV to his
northern capital, an event which Crabbe celebrated in
some suitably mediocre verse. Crabbe was caught up in
the endless festivities occasioned by the King's visit;
and on one famous occasion was found by his
astonished host 'discoursing in execrable French to
some highland chiefs whose costume and Gaelic had

suggested some indefinite foreign origin' (*Dictionary of National Biography*).

Whether or not Crabbe was actually working on *The Voluntary Insane* while in Edinburgh, is impossible to say. He was certainly writing verse at this time. He told his son George on 9 August that he found 'Time in all this Confusion to walk & even rhyme', and that he was planning to bring out another volume.

It is perhaps significant that the nightmare recorded in Crabbe's London Journal for 21 July 1817, which I have already discussed in some detail, happened after an evening spent in the highest and most agreeable of company:

> I returned late last night, and my reflections were as cheerful as such company could make them, and not, I am afraid, of the most humiliating kind.

What this convoluted sentence means is that Crabbe had enjoyed an evening of flattery. He had been lionised as a literary celebrity. This, combined with opium, and, no doubt, plenty of food and drink, seems to have been midwife to the nightmare, bringing it on by means of a sort of opposite and equal reaction: 'Awake, I had been with the high, the apparently happy . . . Asleep, all was misery and degradation . . .'.

Crabbe was also lionised – even more so – during his Edinburgh visit. Sir Walter made sure he was introduced to the leading literary figures in the capital. Adulation was washed down with plenty of alcohol. He told his son he had enjoyed 'Wine & Music & more than I can or perhaps ought to tell you in a Letter'. And of course he was still taking his opium. Judging from the evidence of the London Journal, his 'misery and degradation' – those handmaidens of *The Voluntary Insane*—could have had no better breeding ground.

All this is of course the merest guesswork. But there is one anecdote relating to this time that has a quite uncanny resonance; and a bearing on both the world of Crabbe's dreams and the world of his poetry, the two worlds brought together in *The Voluntary Insane*.

When the son was gathering material for his father's biography, he was supplied by Sir Walter's son-in-law, John Gibson Lockhart, with an account of Crabbe's stay:

> I recollect that he used to have a lamp and writing materials placed by his bedside every night; and when Lady Scott told him she wondered the day was not enough for authorship, he answered, 'Dear Lady, I should have lost many a good hit, had I not set down, at once, things that occurred to me in my dreams.'

On Hampstead's Breezy Heath

Crabbe composed a good deal of his verse while staying with the Hoares. In a letter of June 1825 he told his son that 'I rhyme at Hampstead with a great deal of facility, for nothing interrupts me but kind calls to something pleasant'. And, as the letters to his son and Mary Leadbeater record, he was in the habit of submitting his compositions to Sarah and her stepmother.

There might well have been an additional bond of sympathy between Crabbe, Sarah and her father. It seems that Samuel Hoare, like Crabbe's wife, suffered from acute depression. In a memoir written the year he died Sarah records:

> He had not been long returned from Norfolk [*circa* 1789], when my father was seized by a nervous affection which greatly alarmed my mother . . . I know not at what period to date the commencement of this great drawback to his happiness. He compared it to St. Paul's thorn in the flesh,

sent to buffet him. It infringed upon every comfort, slackened every exertion, made society fatiguing, and solitude irksome; often converted wholesome food into poison, and the most nauseous drugs into the greatest dainties. Like St. Paul too, he used to say, 'I die daily,' for it continually presented the images of death, and produced its most distressing fears. But here it stopped. It had no power over his understanding—always strong enough to resist the phantoms of imagination, though not to conquer them.

Like the Maiden in the poem, this state 'continually presented images of death' to Sarah's father but 'had no power over his understanding'. He was 'strong enough to resist the phantoms of imagination, though not to conquer them'.

Only a small handful of Crabbe's letters to Sarah survive; but those that do show a keen interest on her part in topics relevant to the poem. One of these discusses religious 'Visitations & Conversions', another 'a curious kind of Hallucination which Miss B. discovers in her Addresses to imaginary Beings'.

The fact that no more of Crabbe's letters to Sarah survive is partly attributable to Wordsworth who, like Crabbe, used to use Heath House as a London base. After Crabbe's death, Sarah was asked by Samuel Rogers if the letters to her could be borrowed for use in the son's biography. She turned to Wordsworth for advice. In a note appended to his 'Extempore Effusion upon the Death of James Hogg', Wordsworth tells us what he advised:

> Crabbe I have met in London at Mr. Rogers's, but more frequently and favorably at Mr. Hoare's upon Hampstead Heath. Every spring he used to pay that family a visit of some length, and was upon terms of intimate friendship with Mrs. Hoare, and still more with her daughter-in-law

Detail of a watercolour by Sarah Hoare of her with her father, Samuel

[*sic*], who has a large collection of his letters addressed to herself. After the Poet's decease, application was made to her to give up these letters to his biographer, that they, or at least part of them, might be given to the public. She hesitated to comply, and asked my opinion on the subject. 'By no means,' was my answer, grounded not upon any objections there might be to publishing a selection from these letters, but from an aversion I have always felt to meet idle curiosity by calling back the recently departed to become the object of trivial and familiar gossip.

In this note Wordsworth goes on to talk of his rambles with Crabbe upon Hampstead Heath and the astonishing knowledge of botany he revealed. In the poem itself, Wordsworth commemorates Crabbe as he remembers him from this time:

> Our haughty life is crowned with darkness,
> Like London with its own black wreath,
> On which with thee, O Crabbe! forth-looking,
> I gazed from Hampstead's breezy heath.

A Forgotten Heirloom

After Crabbe died, Sarah Hoare contemplated bringing out a selection from his works and wrote a short memoir to serve as an introduction. Neither memoir nor selection survives, although she did allow the son to make use of the memoir on condition that her name was not used.

It is also known that at least one other of Crabbe's notebooks was in her hands at the time of his death. She wrote to the son on 22 February 1832: 'I today found a book containing a tale neatly written out and called Esther, how it fell into my hands I know not'. She adds that 'Mr Crabbe asked me for it in the summer; and *intended it for publication*'. But this poem, which is usually identified with 'Hester', written by Crabbe in 1804, was not included among the *Posthumous Tales* of 1834, and had to wait until 1960 to be published.

Other notebooks in Sarah Hoare's possession at Crabbe's death appear to have been returned to the son. Most of these have ended up in the Murray or other archives. It seems probable however that the present notebook never left her possession. Perhaps it was overlooked. Or perhaps she was anxious that *The Voluntary Insane* should be protected from prying eyes. One can only guess.

After her death the notebook appears to have been inherited by her niece, Ellen Pryor, later Toller, daughter of her sister Hannah and Thomas Marlborough Pryor. Ellen Toller left the notebook, together with pictures of Heath House and the snuff-box given by Crabbe to Mrs Hoare, to her nephew, Marlborough Robert Pryor, my great-grandfather. It has since then been passed down the family, its authorship at some point slipping from memory.

Judge Not

The question remains: why was *The Voluntary Insane*, if it is George Crabbe's masterpiece, not published either in his lifetime or in the posthumous collection issued in 1834?

One reason might have been that the poem was far too personal. Sarah Hoare, with her own experience of her father's depressive illness, must have been aware of how it touched on Crabbe's innermost life.

The fact that she accepted Wordsworth's advice regarding Crabbe's letters shows that she was sensitive to the more intrusive aspects of biography. In a letter to the son, she has some forthright comments to make on recent biographers, complaining that 'Moore has tortured poor Lady Byron', expressing horror that Thomas Campbell should have revealed details of Sir Thomas Lawrence's dalliance with the daughters of her friend Mrs Siddons, and accusing John Ayrton Paris of having 'no mercy on the peculiarities of Sir H. Davy'. She adds:

> I know a literary friend of your father's who amused a whole company with a story at his expense, and would probably amuse the public with more such tales were he to write his life.

Someone so averse to biographical revelation would surely not have hurried a tale such as *The Voluntary Insane* into print.

Another, closely-allied, reason might have been that the poem was far too shocking. It is not of course always very easy at the end of the twentieth century to gauge what effect a work published in the 1820s or 1830s might have had on a contemporary readership. But perhaps *Tess of the D'Urbervilles*, which has some points of similarity with Crabbe's poem—as well as sharing something of the same tragic power—might give us some sort of clue. When Hardy's novel was published in 1891 it created a furore among certain sections of the press. That was a full seventy years later. And it could be argued that, when it came to subject matter, Crabbe's poem was more shocking still.

The Voluntary Insane is, after all, the work of a Church of England parson, the esteemed and greatly-loved Rector of Trowbridge, a grandfather of nearly seventy, and one of the most respected poets of the age. The elderly rector's poem describes in extraordinarily graphic and lingering detail, with each nuance and shift of mind faithfully recorded, how a young lady, other-

wise a model of feminine and Christian virtues, persuades herself of the desirability of throttling or pressing to death the bastard child of her uncle—a sickly
babe cast entirely on her mercy, a 'nameless Thing'
(916) that has not yet even received the benefit of
baptism—all for the sake of money; or rather for the
sake of an inheritance which would have been partly
hers anyway. It is, she tells us, not so much the prospect
of losing her inheritance, as the horror of having to
share it with this 'nameless Thing', that finally decides
her.

But her good qualities still shine through. She spins
dreams—and who has not spun similar dreams?—of
using her inheritance for relieving suffering and opposing tyranny. Hers is a bountiful, generous nature; and
she indulges her 'eager Mind'

> With sentiments of growing Love,
> And gracious Deeds to all Mankind . . . (987–8)

Besides, she tells herself, the baby, being so sickly,
would have died anyway. She is merely helping it on its
way.

So she presses the life out of her little cousin.
Terrified of discovery, she then feigns madness to
cover up the murder. She succeeds brilliantly. Everyone feels very sorry for her. But she is plagued by guilt
and horror. She desperately seeks forgiveness. She
calls upon the aid of the Church. She calls upon the aid
of less orthodox preachers. But try as she might she
cannot find true repentance. Once on her deathbed, she
confesses all to the Priest. But to no avail. With her last
breath she calls into question the existence of a merciful
God. And goes to her death unshriven.

All of which is based on the history of the late Mrs
Crabbe, sent mad by the death of her children. And,

having twisted his wife's sufferings into such a sem-
blance of evil, what is the moral that the Rector of
Trowbridge draws?

He contents himself with a single couplet, tacked on
to the end of the tale. And what are we told?

> Judge not—thine own Temptation flee.
> Nor parley with the Strength of Sin—

No judgement is passed. We are as she.

THE
VOLUNTARY
INSANE

Misery

The voluntary-Insane.
misery.
Part 1st.
The Character before.

The Hoare Notebook: titlepage of The Voluntary Insane, *with one of
Crabbe's dried botanical specimens still in place*

I

The Character Before

You cannot then believe the Tale,
    Nor your contemptuous Thoughts disguise;
Yet did I not behold thee pale,
    With fixed Attention in those Eyes?
    'Tis Affectation to despise   5
What has such visible Effect:
    Improbable and senseless Lies,
We coolly and at once reject.

Is all that we have heard in Youth,
    All we in after Time have read—   10
All baseless, groundless, void of Truth;
    Of Folly born, by Fancy bred?
    And, above all, this inward dread
Of something that we fear to see?
    Thou art to thy Opinion wed—   15
But hear, and thou divorced will be.

Thou say'st that none can leave the Tomb
    To visit Earthly Scenes again;
No Spirits from their destined Home
    Review a World they now disdain: 20
    Both Soul and Body must remain
Till Heaven's Command the Pair unite,
    To feel th'inexplicable Pain
Or the ineffable Delight.

49

I will not for the Ghost contend,   25
    But something must supply the Place;
There must be Means that have such End,
    From whence these Wonders we may trace.
    What Notions shall we then Embrace?
But let us hear the Tale Again,   30
    Then calmly let us judge the Case
And thus the latent Truth obtain.

MATILDA was discreet though Young,
    So Men, so Women would Agree.
Take her, her lively Sex among,   35
    A livelier you would seldom see;
    Gentle and calm, if grave yet free;
In Air and Manner, Speech and Dress,
    A Pattern, an Example she;
No Want, no Weakness, no Excess.   40

How calm and quiet was her Mind,
    Her Motions neither quick nor slow;
Her Manners easy, pure, refined,
    Her Spirits in an even flow;
    She knew as much as Ladies know   45
Who read for use and not for fame;
    Her learning was not gained for show,
But well her prudent Mind became.

No treacherous Swain had won her heart
   Then left in Grief the heart he won;   50
With no dear Friend compelled to part,
   She felt forsaken and alone;
      To dismal Thoughts she was not prone,
But sang in Solitude, or read,
      And laughed at Lasses Woe-begone   55
Who dreading, knew not what they dread.

She read of Scenes where Horror dwells,
   Of ghostly Grief the dreadful Tale,
Of Victims shut in Monkish Cells
      Doomed to the Hope-Destroying Bale   60
      Of Prison, where the cheerful Gale
That plays without them never blew;
   She at such Midnight Horrors, pale
At Midnight Reading—never grew.

Such Child a Father would approve,   65
   So mild, compliant, easy, gay;
A Wife like her would fondly love
      An Husband and with Pride display,
      Who would both Reason and obey;
Lovers would woo so fair a Bride,   70
   And those who knew her best would say
They wished not other Friend or Guide.

Romantic Friendships she had none
   Contracted in a sudden Flow
Of Girlish Spirits: bound to One   75
      Who must her Bosom's Secrets know
      And to no mortal Being show
(Though why, no mortal Tongue can tell),
   A Trust dissolving like the Snow
That falling, melted as it fell.   80

THE VOLUNTARY INSANE

Yet friends she had, and they were dear;
   Nature and Habit gave her these
And they were useful, tried, sincere;
   Friends pleasing, whom she loved to please.
   The Household Bond was theirs: the Ease   85
And social Comfort, lent to last
   Through Life, through Error, Pain, Disease:
At Want's Approach; When Want is past.

Want she relieved, but never talked
   Of Cottage Joy or Labour sweet;   90
And when she to the Cottage walked
   It was not pure Content to meet,
   Or see a Group of Children greet
Their Parents with a borrowed Grace;
   She let no Dream her Fancy Cheat,   95
Nor her true Charity misplace.

The Poor, she saw them as they are—
   Repining often, struggling hard
With daily Wants and nightly Care,
   From much that sweetens Life debarred.   100
   With these her Wealth she nobly shared;
This done, she laid the Office by.
   She knew that Want has no Regard
To pitying Wealth's superfluous Sigh.

Religion never was her theme—   105
   To hear her Priest, she took her Pew;
There none could more attentive seem,
   Or more correct when she withdrew.
   She asked no Teacher, 'Is it true?';
She neither questioned or denied,   110
   Nor joined the many or the Few
Who follow a dissenting Guide.

But at her Father's Board she sate,
   Where came his Brothers and his Friends;
They often joined in long debate 115
   To which a Youthful Ear attends:
   Full eagerly the Spirit bends
To Subjects grave like those she heard,
   And doubt that troubles and offends
Touched her—she listened till she feared. 120

II

The Change

Such was that Being whom I knew—
   So lively, lovely, frank and gay:
But now behold!—Her livid Hue,
   And Beauties withering all Away,
   Who never knows one cheerful day; 125
Where sunken Eyes and Looks severe
   Prove her to ceaseless Grief a prey!
Without an Hope, without a Tear.

Unseen by Day, she roams by Night,
   Or by the Cliff that bounds the Sea, 130
Or by the melancholy Light
   Of Elms, where Rooks returning flee;
   Or round the reedy Moat where she
Watches with fixed and troubled Look:
   And there she hopes that none will be 135
To view her Frame by Miseries shook.

THE VOLUNTARY INSANE

She hates the Sun, but when he sinks
   Behind the Hill, she wanders late
In her lone Walks, and there she thinks
   And seems to dwell upon her State,   140
   Her Fall, perhaps, perhaps her Fate;
And where she thinks herself alone
   She seems her Story to relate,
Murmuring in miserable Tone.

She has her Places where she goes   145
   To set her struggling Sorrows free—
They seem Congenial to her Woes:
   She there beholds the restless Sea,
   The marshy Ditch, the one bare Tree
With bending Boughs, the bleak broad Fen—   150
   And these with her sad Mind Agree,
And soothe her when she flies from Men.

Her Manner is no longer kind,
   But still she aids the neighbouring Poor,
And gives with sad but bounteous Mind   155
   All that her Duty bids, and more
   Than ever she was wont before;
Yet gives with Looks of Grief and Pain,
   And holds her late augmented Store
For all but this in high Disdain.   160

Her youthful Friends she now forsakes,
   Save when, by fits of fondness led,
The Hand oft linked in hers she takes
   And Tears from tender thoughts are shed—
   Till by a sudden Impulse led   165
She deeply draws the painful Sigh,
   Like one who mourns some favourite dead,
And longs with Anxious Heart to die.

The Change

There was a dreadful Storm at Sea
   And Bodies strewed the pebbly Shore: 170
'Behold them all from Misery free,
   They feel the Ills of Life no more—
   They are not rich, they are not poor;
They cannot think, they cannot weep:
   Will you their happy State deplore,   175
The lasting, pure, unruffled Sleep?'

And there she views the pale cold Cheek;
   She gazes on the sunken Eye,
The Clayey face, the hollow Cheek;
   And looks on Death, as if to die   180
   Was but a Lover's Wish and Sigh!—
'An Insult is our Dread of him.
   We fear to sink to peace and—weak
And wretched—strive in pain to swim.

Swim, and yet feel the Waters round   185
   And Sharks about us mock our Fear,
And some inflict the dreaded Wound—
   But still the wretched Life is dear.
   A thousand ugly Sights appear
And Terrors to our Danger give;   190
   Yet, as our only Friend is near,
We pray like Idiots—"Let us live."'

She loves the burial Earth to tread
   On new-dug Graves, alone to go
To hold strange Converse with the dead,   195
   To Every living Thing a foe;
   'Ah! spend not Life,' they counsel, 'so—
Come to the Friend who loves thee best.'
   She Answers with Derision, 'No!
Here is my Friend, my Hope, my Rest.'   200

THE VOLUNTARY INSANE

Yet are her Sense and Reason clear,
   Her Words are all correct, though few;
Her Sentiments, although severe,
   Are to her own Conceptions true;
   She has no Fancies wild and new,   205
No crazed Enthusiastic Flights;
   She does what she Designs to do:
Though done, in nothing she delights.

Pity she from her Youth displayed;
   To every feeling Creature kind,   210
Attention to their Wants she paid:
   She helped the Insect which the Wind
   Bore to the Brook, and she inclined
Her hand to save the sinking Fly;
   She fed the Raven that was blind,   215
Nor let the captive Dormouse die.

For then she looked on Death with Dread,
   Happy as Birds or Insects then;
She shuddered when she saw the Dead,
   Borne on the Bier by grieving Men: 220
   Oft to the Cottage on the Fen,
On frozen Earth in freezing Air,
   She walked to bear her Comforts when,
And where, she looked to find Despair.

She has been seen to meet a Child   225
   Who could not fear from her Alarms,
For she with Look and Language mild
   Would take it fondly in her Arms,
   As if to shield it from all harms
That Infants share—The child she takes   230
   And in her feverish Bosom warms
And seems to feel the Peace she makes.

Yet then when Tears begin to flow
   And softening Sorrow yields Relief,
She starts as one condemned to know   235
   That she is doomed to endless Grief;
   This checks the Comfort, sad and brief,
And with a Groan she reassumes
   Her Sternness, spurning all Relief,
That came, but now no longer comes.   240

She oft appears to turn about
   And marks some Being who attends,
Oft wildly looks as if in doubt
   Whether to call in Aid her Friends,
   When Terror to her Footsteps lends   245
Unwonted Pace, till Fancies new
   To this bewildered Being sends
Fresh Grief, her Spirit to subdue.

But that all-cheering Favour shown
   To all who suffer, all who may,   250
Is now no more: her Love o'erthrown
   By Grief, she sees the Wretch, a prey
   To many Woes; and turns Away
With angry Features, that imply
   'Would I were half so blest as they   255
Who thus lament, but fear to die.'

Yes, she at Misery looks unmoved,
   She views th'expiring with an Eye
Of one who in her Heart reproved
   The Tears of Friends lamenting by;   260
   And when she hears the tender sigh,
Her stern and ghastly Smiles express
   Contempt of all who fear to die
And bear to linger in Distress.

The Drawings of her favourite Flowers,   265
   The Sounds that from her Chords she drew,
Once solace of her Leisure hours,
   Now painful to her feelings grew;
   Her Letters in the flames she threw,
Yet grieved, but said 'My Fate demands!';   270
   But read and dwelt upon a few,
Then wept and cast them from her hands.

III

Explanation

'And what the Cause?'
              We cannot tell.
   We know the One that she assigns;
What they affirm who with her dwell;   275
   What from her, neighbouring Divines
   Obtained—though much our Priest repines,
Good Man, for sharp and angry Speech,
   When he from his exhaustless Mines
And Stores of Truth, began to preach.   280

But for the Cause—th'unhappy Maid,
   Whose Pains we mourn, Whose fate we dread,
A Visit to some Cousin paid:
   And there an Infant on its Bed
   Saw dying, when alone! and this has led   285
To all that now disturbs and grieves.
   For, since that Day, the Spirit of the Dead!—
The Form attends her! Nor an Instant leaves!

She sat and knew not Death was there;
   But when again her Friends she met,   290
They saw in her distracted Stare
   The Child has paid its Nature's debt!
   She felt it then, she feels it yet!—
While they themselves have ceased to grieve:
   For how shall Mortal Maid forget   295
A Being whom she cannot leave?

To her alone the Shape appears
   To her!—with Friends and Neighbours by—
The Infant's ghastly Look it bears,
   As then in pain, as soon to die!   300
   On her is fixed its feeble Eye,
With deadly wild Expression fraught;
   By her is heard its feeble Cry,
As if it some Compassion sought.

'O! this is Madness'—
               'So indeed!'   305
   We said!—'but how then so serene
Were she, from this one Error freed?'
   I know not Mind so clear and clean
   Of Madness, not a Mark is seen;
To her on any Subject speak: 310
   She is, as she has ever been,
Not wild, nor vain, nor rash, nor weak.

Not long this Infant had expired
   Who thus her vacant Mind surprised,
But she was by some friends desired   315
   To hear a Preacher highly prized
   In his own Walk, who had chastised
The Free-will Folk with burning Zeal!
   'Go Dear,' they said, 'and be advised
And for some greater Object feel.—'   320

THE VOLUNTARY INSANE

So! at the Preacher's feet she stood—
  She who had fled from Reasoners mild—
To hear him talk of flesh and Blood
  By Nature tainted and defiled;
  To hear him say the New-born Child   325
Is doomed to ever-during flame
  Unless—so Fancy was beguiled,
Before enlightening Reason came.

'O! then,' she cried, with Dread oppressed!
  'That wailing Thing is doomed to pain—   330
I saw it sink, but not to rest.
  To me it comes and will remain:
  O! can I peace for it obtain,
Or for my troubled Spirit? No!
  I try, but Trial is in vain—   335
This Man of God proclaims it so.

How dares a mortal sinful Man
  Say as from God what is not true?
"It is decreed," he says, "and can
  Man's feeble power Decrees undo?"   340
  O! horrid Crime, to give such View,
If Heaven did not that View impart:
  That Man, that his meek Brother slew,
Had not so hard, so cold an Heart.'

She tells, nor deviates in her Tale,   345
  That go wherever she wills, this thing,
This bloated Infant, wan and pale,
  Noiseless and moved as on the Wing,
  Will with her move—will to her cling
Th'attendant Curse! All this she states,   350
  And tells that Night nor Sleep can bring
Repose!—nor Day the stubborn Woe abates!

She even loves, 'tis sometimes said,
    To dwell upon her dismal fate,
And seems no longer now afraid   355
    Her first-born Terrors to relate!—
    And how they rose—'Alone I sate,
And saw the vital Spirits Waste,
    Thinking, "So I must meet my Fate,
So I the bitter Cup must taste."   360

None, I observe, were watching by,
    Yet knew how soon the Change must be:
Was it not Cruel, so to fly
    And let the View devolve on me?
    A Spirit struggling to get free!   365
O! what an Eye to gaze on mine;
    That saw, and could no longer see,
That shone, and must no longer shine.'

'And can such Common Fate my Child,'
    A Matron said, 'give such Distress   370
To One like you, so clear, so mild?'—
    'Chide, Chide me not!' she cried! 'Repress!
    Both your Reproof and Tenderness!
Think you my Will such Pangs would feel?
    Think you I would the Ills caress—   375
That I would give a World to heal?

I tell you what mine Eyes have seen:
    The Spirit of the Dead;—no Night,
Nor curtaining Darkness ever screen
    That Image! And it braves the Light!   380
    Lo! Now this instant, in my Sight,
It mocks me! saying, "Thou shalt die";
    I slighted Truth, but can I slight
A Warning that is Ever by?'

THE VOLUNTARY INSANE

There was a reverend Priest and learned, 385
 If not discreet, and he would pray
With Her, for whom his Bowels yearned,
 And he would drive the foe Away—
 Alas! the best that He could say,
Her Indignation raised, and Spleen; 390
 And he regrets—Good Man!—the day
When he encountered One so keen.

He talked of God's Decrees, As one
 Consulted in th'important Case;
He told her all that had been done 395
 By, for, and with her fallen Race;
 Talked of the mighty power of Grace
For which in vain the Lost may try;
 And then, with Heart of Flint and face
Unmoved, said!—'Art thou fit to die?' 400

He said that those redeemed by Grace
 Had not a Merit to display,
And those condemned—th'accursed Race—
 Had as much real Worth as they;
 For neither had a Mite to pay: 405
But this was Mercy to receive,
 And this is lost—'Believe who may—'
She cried—'I cannot that believe.

And does thy priestly Pride delight
 In wringing thus the human heart? 410
Who gave thee, impious Man, a Right
 Thy Councils as thy God's t'impart?
 Sinful and ignorant thou art;
And Evil dreading, yet would bring
 Evil on us, and Give the Dart 415
Of Death a tenfold power to sting!

Explanation

O! the Profession is a Cheat,
  And that the grave Impostors know:
To you for Refuge we retreat,
  And this you promise to bestow;   420
  You promise, but to you we owe
Tidings that aggravate our Grief!
  Life's common Comforts you o'erthrow,
And give its Sorrows no relief.

Lo! the poor Indian who has done   425
  What Nature prompted him to do;
Soon as he feels his Race is run,
  He takes of Life no sad Review;
  But hopes what he is told is true:
That he shall happier Climes possess,   430
  Where he shall nobler Game pursue,
And his Privations will be less.

Go cruel thou, and tell the Wretch
  Who in her Bed of Torture lies
That Hope her weary wings must stretch,   435
  And from far distant clouded Skies
  Bring Comfort, Faith's precarious Prize,
Whereto she sets her mystic Seal;
  And if she feel it not, she dies.
I feel it not—I cannot feel.'   440

'Thou hast been reading, O! my Child,
  And Reading is a dangerous Thing.
By Books what Numbers are beguiled—
  And all indeed, but those who bring
  A mind that Heavenward loves to spring,   445
And feels th'Adoption! O! had'st thou
  That Song for thine, the Ransomed sing—
But O! what thy Condition now?'

63

THE VOLUNTARY INSANE

'How vain, how insolent,' the Maid
    Returned, 'How great, how mean, the Pride   450
That strives to make the Soul afraid
    And then profess to be its Guide;
    To dole out Hopes and fears, decide
On Doubts, and pains of Mind remove;
    And make us all at length confide   455
In Teachers whom we cannot love.

But come, your Counter Charm apply—
    There is a Spectre in my View:
Lo!—now'; the Preacher turned his Eye
    On nothing—'Maiden, bid Adieu   460
    To Dreams so impious, and pursue
The good, the right, the pious Way;
    And join the Elect, the precious few,
Who weep and fast, and watch and pray.'

'Agreed! But make this fiend depart,   465
    And I will then thy Creed profess!—
Will strive to break the flinty Heart!—
    To kill Despair, will court Distress:
    But Go! and every hope Suppress
To give me Comfort! Yes! Be gone—   470
    Thou canst not make, nor more nor less
The mighty Power that Drives me on.

Go mount thy Tub and take thy Text,
    And Cry to every Wanderer near;
Talk on, nor think of what comes next;   475
    Be bold, be loud, be most severe:
    Prove you to Hell their Title clear—
At least Assert! For that is Proof,
    And they will hold you very dear,
And think they cannot praise enough.   480

Leave me—' she cries impatient, then
   Laments the Scorn she so conveyed,
For she dislikes the Sight of Men!
   In part displeased, in part afraid,
   She sometimes utters, 'I'm betrayed!'   485
When some grave Preacher comes to find
   What passes with th'unhappy Maid,
How works the melancholy Mind.

Now judge you; is she or not insane?
   Soundness you see in all beside;   490
Is it the Mind's strong Foe, the Bane
   Of human Reason, human Pride?
   You may in what she says confide,
You may to her your Doubts propound;
   But for that Daemon at her Side—   495
Who is more rational and sound?

Is it in Nature that the Brain
   Should be of such Disease the Prey,
As will this Circumstance explain?
   Going in just one thought astray—   500
   Erring in just that single Way—
By that as in a Tempest tossed,
   Without Direction, Night and Day;
By that confounded, led and lost.

Such is my Story, nothing new   505
   Has risen—mysterious still the Thing:
I know not in what Light to view
   A Tale, nor how some Truth to bring
   In such Confusion! What can spring
From such Relation?—We in vain   510
   Exert our Reason; Doubts will Cling
To us; and with us still Remain—.

You think it Madness? O! but then
    Think with what Sense, and how sedate;
Think with what ready Mind and Pen   515
    She can her every Purpose state,
    And all that you require relate:
She does what sounder Minds will do,
    Remembers every Place and Date,
And can Life's Every Act review—.   520

IV

Conference

Two years had passed; The Maid was yet
    Alive, but sinking to the Grave—
Willing to pay her Nature's debt,
    But not her Judge, her God, to brave
    By casting off the Life he gave: 525
She waited eager!—not resigned;
    Nor Ease, nor Hope, nor Health would crave—
Rest, Rest alone she wished to find.

The Priest here
'I sometimes saw her; Of her Pain
    The now Enfeebled Sufferer spoke—   530
"Think not that I your Help disdain,"
    She said, "but vainly you invoke
    The Aid of Heaven: I bear the Stroke
Of Adverse Fate, and I must bear—
    And your Religion is a Yoke   535
That my free Soul disdains to wear."

I sought my Purpose to unfold
    And spoke of Heaven's all powerful Aid,
But she to this was deaf and cold;
    Her Misery no Attention paid   540
    To Mercy, such as I conveyed,
But bade me go in fretful tone—
    I heard with Pity and obeyed,
And left the indignant Maid alone.

I sometimes saw her when a Smile   545
    Severe presided in her Look:
Keen and sarcastic then her Style,
    Nor could she Admonition brook;
    Yet when her Pain and Anger spoke
In words severe, her Spirit felt   550
    Her Frailty!—Scorn her Heart forsook,
And softness in her Features dwelt.

It was that fancied Being viewed
    By Fear, by Terror at her Side;
It was that Teacher, stern and rude,   555
    Who Threat'ning in her Case applied;
    It was that harsh relentless Guide,
Who planted Terror in her Breast:
    Who to her Soul, the Peace denied
That his elected Crew possessed.   560

"'Believe' they say!—why more believe,
    To give new horrors to my Lot?
If Grace I am not to receive,
    Better that I believe it not—
    Let this sad Doctrine be forgot   565
And changed for that eternal Sleep;
    And let me from my Memory blot
The Truths that I am Cursed to keep.

THE VOLUNTARY INSANE

I have not Faith, I have not Grace
  Your pleasant Doctrines to admit: 570
Why should I then the ill embrace?
  Why if for better things unfit
  Should I, condemned, expectant sit?
I know not what of Ill ordained,
  I know not why!—far better quit   575
All Thought, than think what Priests have feigned."

It was not easy to reply
  To One so lost, and I had Awe
Of one who wished and dared to die,
  Pleased from Existence to withdraw;   580
  I had seen nothing, nothing saw,
For so much agonising Pain—
  I knew there was the righteous Law!—
But how it bore, could not explain.

Still I of Comfort spoke, "Dear Maid,   585
  The Offered Blessing why refuse?
Thy Father bids, be not afraid;
  He bids thy Trust, and do not Lose
  Such Hope and such delightful Views
As Love and Mercy now present;   590
  Believe, it is with thee to choose—
O! be not hard of Heart—relent."

She was not softened, but a fear
  Upon her Mind would sometimes steal;
I spoke of Judgment—"Be sincere: 595
  Wouldst thou to Justice strict appeal?"
  "Not so; but canst thou More reveal?
Must I the Mercy court or lose?
  Have I not said I cannot feel!—
Then wilt thou tell me, I can choose?   600

68

And tell me truly, is there Proof
   On which a Mortal may rely?
And is there Evidence enough
   That dying, we not all shall die?
   'Tis Nature's wish, 'tis Nature's Cry   605
That something shall of us remain—
   That thinking, reasoning being, I—
Of this I think, and think in vain.

You say the Accepted shall rejoice,
   You say the wicked howl in Woe,   610
That some shall hear the heavenly Voice,
   And some to Seats of Torment go
   With our Seducer, and Heaven's Foe:
A Nursery Tale on Babes impressed—
   Can I believe it?—No no no: 615
The Living die!—The Dead have Rest."

"Peace, and be sure that God is just."
   "And who is he that says 'Be sure'?
Here I must be, because I must;
   Must breathe and languish, and Endure—   620
   And who, Alas!, these Ills shall Cure?
Death—and how cruel then are you
   To worry Minds unclean, impure,
With Dread of Evils to ensue.

'Tis but Discourse—When all is well,   625
   And when our Days and Prospects Shine,
We in our lighter Spirits dwell
   On Providence and Power divine;
   But as our Better Hopes decline,
And heavier, darker Days advance,   630
   We at our gloomy Views repine,
And talk of Fortune, Fate, and Chance."

"Nay! think it not, for Man is tried
   And proved in his Existence here;
Here chastened, and his Wish denied;   635
   Here feels the Pang, and sheds the Tear:
   And does not this to you Appear?
Think you some Power above at Will
   Inflicts Pains useless and severe,
As Flies the wanton Children kill?   640

The Dog whom with our Hands we feed
   Is therefore dearer in our Eyes;
We for our Service train the Steed,
   And thence of greater Value prize
   All that we train, in Worth arise   645
And we the different Rate decide:
   And shall the mighty Power that tries
The Heart of Man, forget it tried?—"

"If Life be Trial, I have failed,"
   She said, "and cannot further try."   650
"Repentance, Lady, has prevailed!—
   Conviction's Pain, Reflection's Sigh!
   Thou canst not have such Cause!—Apply
Ev'n if thou hast! and Heaven implore!"
   She paused!—"No more!—but let me fly   655
These wearing Dreams! and think no more."

"One moment"—"No! not one," she cried,
   "But O! there might have been a Day
When I so sweetly might have died
   An Infant, in the Lap at play—   660
   One Grasp had squeezed my Life Away;
Or at the Worst, some friendly blow
   Had placed me with my Kindred Clay!—
That cannot think, fear, feel, or know."

It would be tedious Pain to tell   665
   The Conflict of a smitten Heart;
I will not on that Warfare dwell,
   Nor will the useless Strife impart:
   I've seen her for an Instant start,
As by some strong Emotion led,   670
   Then call for Death, and urge the dart
And talk with Envy of the dead.

A Friend who once to her was dear
   Said, "Dost thou now that Being see?
Surely it cannot now appear,   675
   Or would it all be lost on me?"
   "Ask not!" she cried, "how this can be:
Thy Fate is not like mine severe—
   Art thou its Object? Well for thee,
Thou art not. Go, and leave us here.   680

The Wind blows where it lists, and Hell
   Sends forth its Legions uncontrolled,
As far as you or I can tell;
   And I to one fierce Fiend am sold—
   There now it glides, behold, behold!   685
No! thou art happy not to see—
   Those shadowy Arms shall not enfold
Thy Form—Hell's Love is not for thee.

Nay grieve not, be not thou appalled:
   Thine is no singular Distress—   690
Thou art not by a Daemon called,
   Art not the Spouse of Wretchedness—
   No unclean Spirit is thy Guest,
That to thy shuddering bosom brings
   Strange wicked thoughts that none confess,   695
Thoughts of abominable Things . . ."

71

THE VOLUNTARY INSANE

Days, Months and Seasons passed Away,
  And nothing I beheld or heard;
I missed her in her Haunts by day,
  By night no longer she appeared: 700
  By our tall Cliff the Coaster steered,
Her Voyage unmarked by us on shore;
  I know not what I thought or feared—
Was she, or were her Griefs, no more?

At Length I heard Disease had worn   705
  The Mind and Body: it had won
The stronger Forts of Life, had torn
  The fragile System and had done
  All that Affliction can; to shun
The Grave was hopeless!—"Hope," she Cried,   710
  "To that dear Goal with Joy I run—
If certain, then I need no Guide."

It was upon that dying Bed
  Where pale she laid, and cold as clay;
Dreading she knew not what to dread,   715
  And praying for a Heart to pray,
  I saw her in that gloomy day—
And spoke of Love divine; and Love
  Lent to the struggling Mind a Ray
Of Light!—and with her Terror strove.   720

It broke upon that horrid Cloud,
  And caused a plenteous flow of Tears;
She wept, and long she wept aloud;
  Wept, and laid open all her fears,
  And felt the mighty Storm that clears   725
The cloudy Mind!—The pains that prove
  There is a gracious Power, that hears
Such Cry!—The power of heavenly Love.

"Sit," she began! "and thou shalt hear,
  If I have strength!—and let me try   730
That I am, not what I appear.
  I would not in Deception die,
  Nor leave a spotless Name, a Lie.
For that would be the greater Sin—
  But is there none—Come near me!—by?—   735
O! Pride!—When I my Tale begin . . .

Was I not—Thou rememberest well,
  With all in Estimation high?
Even now, to my Reproach, they tell
  How lovely, how beloved was I: 740
  The Cause they said of many a Sigh,
But kindly grieving for the Pain—
  That fled!—it seems—when I was by,
If so—Alas! it came again.

They called me fair, and I could smile   745
  Softly, as modest Maid behoved;
I wrote, and Men approved the Style,
  And meekly I the Praise approved;
  I heard of all my Charms unmoved:
That Fame had little Weight with me—   750
  But I had Views, and dearly loved
To hear how wealthy I must be.

73

THE VOLUNTARY INSANE

How strange to you it must appear,
    An Infant Soul could have the Taint
Of Avarice, but I am Sincere;   755
    And had I Words at will, could paint
    That strong Corruption! But how faint
Are Words, that Evil to deplore—
    How early was it my Complaint,
That, having much, I had no more.   760

This darling Sin was ever fed
    By all that I observed or saw,
By all that I conceived or read:
    It seemed an everlasting Law
    That Riches kept Mankind in Awe—   765
I dreamed of Jewels, Garments, Gold:
    All that admiring Crowds would draw,
That they would with Desire behold!

I heard them speak of wealthy Men,
    So close, so fond of what they gain,   770
That like a Lion in his Den
    They in their District proudly reign,
    And more than sovereign State maintain:
While thousands sigh, for but a Part
    Of their vast Store! Alas, in vain   775
I strove!—the wish possessed my Heart.

I heard with eager Joy the Sum
    Bequeathed to me, a simple Child:
Mine would my Father's Wealth become;
    I heard! and (ah! deceit) reviled   780
    The Thought! And thus were they beguiled—
''Twas Joy, such Spirit to behold!'—
    And on the Baby-Miser smiled
Who had (they thought) such Scorn of Gold.

Thus hard of Heart, of Spirits light,   785
   I seemed free, generous, and kind;
My Fortune ever in my Sight,
   The Means for ever in my Mind:
   My wealthy Friends were sure to find
Me all Attentive, but they knew   790
   No Ill in this; but all were blind
To that vile Love, and how it grew.

One who had more than All beside,
   Gained in the Still-productive East,
Was pleased with one so much allied   795
   In Thought, and my Desire increased:
   He taught me how my Soul to feast
On Bonds and Parchments, and would say:
   'My Wife, my Children, are deceased;
But thou . . .', then weeping turn Away.   800

I let him weep, and kindly sighed—
   Who could so young a Lass suspect?
'Thou hast a tender Heart' he cried,
   And for my Sake his Sorrow checked.
   His Life was hitherto correct—   805
A Man grave, prudent, thoughtful, still:
   Few Things his Passions could effect;
His Reason ever swayed his Will.

But he had Sin, and that was seen
   By a Domestic, shrewd and fly,   810
Light, and alluring, crafty-kind;
   With careless Air, with wanton Eye,
   And Manner that would much imply
To him who doubted in his Mind;
   That seemed to say, 'You can but try,   815
And you shall no Repulsion find.'

75

THE VOLUNTARY INSANE

And none he found . . . Then all of mine,
 All that rejoiced my heart before,
All that I held, I must resign
  To that unlawful Heir she bore: 820
  Their Crime—not that I mourned, but sore
My Grief for my dear Prospects fled;
 Those Bonds, those Lands were mine no more;
My Hopes were lost, were dying, dead.

My Uncle soothed me and was kind,   825
 The Woman humble; so I went,
Sullen at first, but I designed
  At their Entreaty to relent;
  But secret kept the favour meant:
While he most bounteous Presents made,   830
 Nor heeded what he largely spent,
Me into Kindness to persuade.

The Child was sick, nor seemed to love
 The World to which he came of late;
And while the Mother fondly strove   835
  T'avert, she met her Infant's fate:
  As with the Wailing Boy she sate,
Languid and pale and faint she grew;
 Ate not, slept ill, and mourned her State,
And from her daily Cares withdrew.   840

Then breathed with Labour and in Pain,
 And bitter Tears, repenting shed;
And shunned with Fear, and with Disdain,
  What to familiar Converse led:
  She languished by her Boy, one bed   845
Held whom it seemed one Grave must hold—
 And soon we saw the Mother dead,
And then the Infant's fate foretold!

The Child was sick nor seemed to love
The World to which he lately came
And while the mother fondly strove
To avert, she met the Infants fate
As with the wailing Boy she sate
Languid pale & faint she grew
Eat not, slept ill, mourned her state
And from her daily Cares withdrew

Then breathed with Labour & in pain
And bitter Tears, repenting shed
And shunned with Fear & with Disdain
What to familiar Sorrow led
She languished by her Boy, one bed
Held whom it seemed one grave must hold
And soon we saw the Mother dead
And then the Infants fate foretold

Grieved I not then? I wept; the Child
Of a sad Father seemed my own
Yet then a thought, an Hope beguiled
My Heart whose wish was never known
From that hard heart as God was known
All Woman's nature I caressed
The Babe upon my Kindness thrown
And what I felt repelled, repressed

The Hoare Notebook: page of the manuscript of The Voluntary Insane
lines 833–856, with dried botanical specimen in place

Grieved I not then? I wept; the Child
　　Of a sad Father seemed my Own!　　　　　　850
Yet then a Thought, an Hope beguiled
　　My Heart, whose Wish was never known:
　　From that hard Heart, ah! God!—was flown
All Woman's Nature! I caressed
　　The Babe upon my Kindness thrown—　　　855
And what I felt? repelled, repressed!

You look, Alas!, with earnest Eye:
　　What is it you can yet perceive?
'Have I confessed?', your Looks reply:
　　But do not more than truth believe.　　　860
　　'Tis not as you suppose—I grieve
For what it is; but come, attend—
　　I cannot your Esteem retrieve
But, Man of God! my Soul befriend.

Ah! What Contention have I felt—　　　865
　　'And will he leave it all?' I cried,
'It is his own—His Heart will melt,
　　When he is by its pleadings tried.
　　Law and his Niece then set aside,
He to that Being, all will give—　　　870
　　O! would that shivering Thing had died,
But he will pine and feed, and live.'

Your Looks reprove me, yet indeed
　　'Tis Nature—Now the Babe declined:
The Father said, 'It is decreed,　　　875
　　I thus my Punishment shall find;
　　It was my Sin, I am resigned—'
He was—Alas, so was not I.
　　Nor in my Heart could Pity find
For One who would not quickly die.　　　880

Convulsed the pale cold boy became—
  'Gone! he is gone' the Father cried,
'O! bury with him Sin and Shame'—
  'Bury your Sorrow.' I replied,
  Peevish!—for I the Life espied,   885
Rekindling—'He, an happy Boy,
  Will by your Hoards and Lands be tried,
That He, not you, will then enjoy.'

And now returned the frequent Fit,
  O'erpowering Sense, enduring long,   890
While I beside him bore to sit,
  Indulging Thoughts, a dreadful Throng;
  But chief, of Riches gained by wrong!
And what is wrong, where all would gain?
  And then I saw Life growing strong!   895
And reddening in the Cheek Again!

Thus was Vexation, Trouble, Pain,
  Trial and Torment, wearing all
My Spirits, when I saw Again
  The shake, the fit, the chilling call   900
  Of Death—and then the creeping small
Reviving Pulse Again would beat:
  Again to rise, Again to fall,
And my impatient Hope to cheat.

Then Nature made an Effort new,   905
  The Life precarious to prolong;
The Father came the Child to view
  And saw the misborn being strong:
  Then sang he, fool he was, his Song
Of Thanks, that set my Soul a Snare . . .   910
  'Niece! I must do my Boy no Wrong,
But thou shalt in the Savings share!'

Share! What? The Scraping of the Board?
   Share of the Gleanings—and with One
Whom I have fondled, nursed, restored?   915
   The nameless Thing he calls his Son?
   Imprudent Care! but I must shun
Such Thoughts! and would my Mind were freed—
   But come they will!—I cannot run
From Thought!—but will not name the Deed.   920

Do I Offend You, or affright?
   Alas, you look not now the Friend—
May we not wish ourselves a Right?
   And may we not our Rights defend?
   Heaven! Do not Men in Battle spend   925
Blood!—and destroy when they might save:
   And do not all our Passions send
Their groaning Myriads to the Grave?

Hope, when deferred too long, destroys;
   Fear, Sorrow and Despair will kill;   930
Love bears away our Girls and boys,
   And Hatred lives Men's blood to spill:
   Where is the Medicine, where the Skill
That can the Soul's Disorders tame?
   There lives within, the growing ill   935
That leads to Death, the wasting Frame—

Quickly their Way the Passions Win—
   And Reason's slumbering Guard destroy:
My Uncle's Folly sought the Inn—
   To talk of his recovered Boy   940
   And drench the Clowns in drunken Joy;
Him followed Men and Maids—I sate
   In Angry Silence—My Employ
To watch the Cause and weep my Fate.

Sudden! the Bells with horrid Peal   945
   Rang out! Malicious Idiots, Why?
Wretches! Did I in Magic deal,
   The Ropes about your Necks should fly
   And every Hound be drawn on high,
That not one Hand a Rope should take   950
   To wake this Creature sleeping by—
Or fatal thoughts in me to wake.

They rang; my Head confused, my Heart
   Grew wrathful, and it grieved and bled,
And that pale Boy began to start!—   955
   And grew convulsed upon his Bed;
   His Eye rolled wildly, and his head
Some strong spasmodic Force obeyed;
   Then rested!—'Ah! and is he dead?
Is mine, is nature's Debt thus paid?'   960

Hope, Joy and Wonder forged a Chain
   That bound my Soul! Within my Chair
I watched—'He cannot come Again'—
   I formed a selfish, sinful Prayer:
   I tried his Breath! the unmoved Air   965
Stirred not the Feather's Down; I drew
   Near the Wan Life—'No more despair'
I said in Joy!—'vile Fears Adieu!'

Alas!—and must I now proceed?
   I sat, and not a Being by—   970
Thoughts came—If asked who did the Deed?
   'I did it not,' I could reply.
   Then should the boy breathe yet?—O! why
Could I not still without a Fear
   Do that? And yet that done deny? . . .   975
O! mercy, look not so severe!

'Why, then suppose'—I thought—'suppose
   He had not died, and I had pressed? . . .'
You say I must the Truth disclose,
   Locked like a fire within my Breast.   980
   Suppose this Being's happy Rest
Had been by me?—who would conceive
   That I that Spirit dispossessed?
That I . . . No Creature could believe.

My Joy was still. I could not move,   985
   But I indulged an eager Mind
With Sentiments of growing Love,
   And gracious Deeds to all Mankind:
   I would enjoy Delight refined,
I would all Tyranny oppose;   990
   And had some twenty Plans designed,
For easing Pains and chasing Woes.

Self-soothed by this, th'accursed deed
   Stole with my Boastings to my Breast;
As yet—for Strength, I saw no Need;   995
   None for Resistance; I had Rest,
   And all was good!—The Hour so blest
Its Quiet to the Bosom gives.
   Nay, Nay! That Clod is repossessed!
It moves!—it breathes, it looks!—it lives!   1000

But wilt thou come Again, wilt thou
   Me of my prospects dispossess?
Does Life rekindle thus, and how
   Can I with mockery acquiesce?
   There may—there must be—some Redress   1005
For Spirits wrought like mine, I will—
   Strange Rival, let me view thee—Yes!
We must our Destiny fulfil.

I looked and saw no Creature nigh,
   And then again returned to view   1010
The half unsealed and cloudy Eye,
   That shut again; for Life was new,
   Not perfect Life—I could not do
A Deed so foul; I had not planned
   To shut out Life, if fair and true: 1015
But this . . . O! Why so drop my Hand?

In Pity spare me—I have felt
   Unintermitting, day and Night,
Remorse and Horror, God has dealt
   Me Pangs for Sin!—'tis just, 'tis right,   1020
   Condemn not thou! but in his Sight
Thou, too, art faulty—let me live
   As one whom her own thoughts affright:
Sinner thyself, my Sin forgive.

O! it was vile, but Life indeed,   1025
   Though kindling, was not come—the breast
Moved not—though Motion might succeed.
   'It will not die!' I said, and pressed . . .
   My God forgive . . . and it had rest,
That I from that accursed time   1030
   Never, in one sweet Hour, possessed:
So sure does Misery wait on Crime.

I gazed on that still Clay and cried
   'It is not Murder—He was dead
Or dying, nay he must have died.   1035
   Then what have I for this to dread?'
   I turned me from th'accursed Bed,
And the approaching Father saw!
   Then Comfort, and then Courage fled;
And Him I feared, and feared the Law.   1040

THE VOLUNTARY INSANE

A Court of Justice came in View,
  My Trial and the Sentence passed:
And from th'appalling Scene I drew
  My Self-Possession, and I cast
  My Thoughts around!—and though Aghast   1045
At so much Danger and distress,
  I sought Expedients, and at last—
'Thus will I do! And this profess—'

Then rushed as Maddened from the Scene,
  And met the Father as he came—   1050
'Ah! What does all this Terror mean'
  He cried, 'that thus can shake thy frame?
  Niece, my beloved Niece, O! Name
The Cause of such Emotion—Why
  That frightened Air? Those Eyes on flame?   1055
Thy Looks disordered?—O, reply!'

My Part was taken. I must seem
  To be as One whose troubled Breast,
Like those who labour in a Dream,
  Is by insane sad thoughts possessed: 1060
  I will not answer—I am pressed
By Grief too heavy—So I took
  His Hand and held it, and he guessed
The Evil that my Action spoke!

He ran, and all was quickly known;   1065
  He gazed One Moment on the dead
And, having some still Sorrow shown,
  He turned to me, and calmly said
  'Have rest!—behold upon that bed
My Sin and punishment—be still.   1070
  Let me not greater Evil dread,
But bow to the Almighty Will.

84

Ah! my poor Girl, wert thou alone
   When Death this sudden Visit paid?
May for my Guilt, my Grief atone;   1075
   And spare just Heaven this guiltless Maid.'
   O! then indeed I was afraid . . .
But felt that I must persevere:
   So, sullen, Silent, lost, dismayed,
I heard not—Would not seem to hear.   1080

Then Neighbours came; and then the Law
   Sent its Enquiries, how he died;
But nothing heard they, nothing saw;
   They questioned: wildly I replied,
   And they were quickly satisfied—   1085
''Twas Heaven's high Will! His Time, his Date.'
   Then looked on me and pitying Cried,
'Unhappy Lady! dreadful Fate!'

So have I acted; from that Hour,
   Appearing never to regain   1090
My former Self—Without a Power
   My Case correctly to explain!
   My Friends sought kindly to obtain
Peace, Health and Comfort, and they tried
   A thousand gentle Means, in vain—   1095
My Peace with that poor Being died.

Nor from that Moment have I dared
   To meet a Friend, with Mind at rest;
But have to all those Friends declared
   I saw that Being—so it best   1100
   Seemed for me, that I should attest
As frightened, and that dreadful thought
   Upon my troubled Brain impressed,
And in that Day of Horror wrought.

Yet dared I not in much beside   1105
  To seem insane, for well I knew
I might in my Discourse be tried;
  And dreaded to be found untrue—
  I shunned in fear the observing few,
But trusted Folly in the Crowd: 1110
  I kept my first Design in View
And what I then conceived, Avowed.

It was my Purpose to recall,
  Slowly, when safely, reason's Aid;
But as I dreaded Questions all,   1115
  To reason I was still afraid;
  Whoever spake appeared t'upbraid
The Wretch he pitied—so I deemed
  My Safety was the Part I played,
And I was saved by that I seemed.   1120

Then dismal were my Nights, and fraught
  With horrid Visions; in my Dream
I saw my Judge, and Mercy sought;
  I was condemned . . . was then a theme
  For vulgar Scorn and rage; extreme   1125
Was my Distress: the fancied Grief
  Vanished indeed . . . the Morning-beam
Brought Truth, but Truth was not Relief.

When I have heard, and I did hear,
  Rumours, my very blood to freeze,   1130
I studied how myself to clear,
  Brooding on new Designs; and these
  Have made Life loathsome—O! for Ease,
For Sleep profound, from Terrors, Woes:
  From all the guilty Spirit sees;   1135
From all that murders its repose.

Say! from Death's Sleep do we awake—
    And then for Judgment take our Way?
Lo! I am ready to forsake
    All Life can promise, or can pay.   1140
    But if there be that reckoning Day—
There cannot! We are taught Amiss—
    The penalty even now I pay!
This is our World, and only this.

And I do see him: Yes, I see   1145
    That spectre-Infant; Whom I pressed
To stop the Life about to be
    Awakened in the Frame at rest.
    To see that Being I professed,
And I do see him—the Strong Lie   1150
    Has to my guilty Soul possessed,
That I do see him!—Ever by.

I now must die. My haunted Mind
    Cannot the five fold Woe sustain.
This part I act the World to blind,   1155
    And this dire Burden I sustain.
    The Guilt, the Trouble and the Pain
Of Conscience!—Judge! Informer! Spy!
    And this Disease upon the brain—
All are Life's bane! And I must die.   1160

Tell me! but let your Words be true—
    But do you in your Heart maintain
That some strange Power will Life renew,
    And I, this Wretch, shall live Again?
    And shall the Comforter in vain—   1165
Death!—hide me in his quiet Cell?
    Is there a Force to break his Chain,
And rewake Souls to Suffering? . . . tell.

THE VOLUNTARY INSANE

O! I could hearken Once to things
   Our sleepy Rector prosing taught: 1170
Belief from Innocency springs,
   And I had Faith, for Faith I sought;
   But when that Deed of Death I wrought,
That Faith I wanted to expel.
   Now with strange Doubts, the Soul is fraught; 1175
But will there be that Trial?—tell!

This Faith you teach, and this you Strive
   To force on all! as Children play
From Hand to Hand to bear alive
   The idle fire that must decay; 1180
   So you from Mind to Mind convey
This Faith, and all to take agree:
   Not so—for I the forfeit pay.
The trembling fire goes out with me.

Yet may it be . . . perhaps it must. 1185
   Now go! and let my Miseries sleep.
Return! And sacred be the trust:
   It is not long thou hast to keep
   My Secret; why I cannot weep!—
Nor Pray, nor send my Thoughts on high 1190
   Above the Earth!—on which I creep,
The Soil in which I long to lie.

And now farewell! The Power that broke
   The Rock and made the Waters flow
May give the Heart an healing Stroke. 1195
   And I, even I, may Mercy know,
   That He will to the Sufferer show
Who flies to him! Delicious View!
   But I am Cold of Heart—and slow
To that Belief . . . but is it true?"' 1200

My Secret. Why I cannot weep,
nor pray, nor send my Sighs on high
Above the Earth, on which I creep
The Soil in which I long to lie.

And now farewell! The Power that broke
The Rock and made the Waters flow
May give the Heart an healing stroke
And even I may mercy know
That He will to the Sufferer show
Who fly to him! delicious View!
But I am Cold of Heart & slow,
To that Belief ___ but is it true.

Twas Even-tide ___ the Flocks were pen'd
And Shepherds whistled oer the Lee
But eer that Summer Night had End
The Maid was from Life's burden free
Alone she died; no Eye could see
The Signs without of Thoughts within ___
Judge not ___ thine own Temptation flee
Nor parley with the Strength of Sin ___

The Hoare Notebook: page of the manuscript of The Voluntary Insane
lines 1189–1208

THE VOLUNTARY INSANE

'Twas Eventide—the Flocks were penned,
  And Shepherds whistled o'er the Lea;
But e'er that Summer Night had End
  The Maid was from Life's burden free.
  Alone she died; no Eye could see   1205
The Signs without of Thoughts within—
  Judge not—thine own Temptation flee.
Nor parley with the Strength of Sin—

Appendices

I. A Note on the Text

Ideally, I would have liked to print the text of *The Voluntary Insane* in the form left by George Crabbe. Unfortunately this has not been possible.

The text is so lightly punctuated that reading it would have presented a considerable struggle: and it has been my aim, above all, to make the text readily accessible. This is a text aimed at the general reader, rather than the scholar (which I would not be equipped to provide).

I have attempted to preserve Crabbe's punctuation where it does exist, strengthening it where necessary, as this obviously bears directly on how Crabbe wanted the poem read. As any editor of Crabbe will know, exclamation marks have presented special problems. He often used these in the middle of a sentence, almost as a form of underlining; and very often this brings the modern reader to a dead halt, a cue for mopping the brow and admiring the view: where it was Crabbe's intention that he should hurry on. I have tried to preserve as many of these exclamation marks as I can, sometimes by placing a dash after them or, more occasionally, by juggling with their position, or substituting some other mark. Or sometimes by leaving them where they are.

I would also have liked to preserve Crabbe's spelling and usages (e.g. 'blissing' for 'blessing', 'tretcherous' etc.), but have decided to err on the side of accessibility, and have therefore modernised the spelling throughout. I have also expanded ampersands. Sometimes where use of an ampersand contrasts with the use of 'and', it has been possible to reflect this by use of a comma.

I have preserved Crabbe's original capitalisation,

although this is not always consistent. It does however, like his punctuation, reflect rhythm and emphasis. As there is a fair scattering of these, they should not prove a distraction. Where a piece of the manuscript has been cut out and Sarah Hoare has supplied a transcript without capitals, I have supplied my own for the sake of conformity (in one case borrowing from the 'Misery' version).

I am aware that my transcript of the poem is a botched compromise, and would have remained so however long I spent tinkering with it. I console myself with the thought that, however bad it might be, it never need be the last word; and that if ever a new edition is called for, another editor or editors will greatly improve upon it. It is an interim report only. But as 173 years have already been allowed to elapse, I thought it time *The Voluntary Insane* finally saw the light of day.

II. Textual Variants

At several points Crabbe has added an alternative reading, without deleting the original, leaving us with a choice of text. These and other points of interest (excluding superseded readings) are as follows:

41–8 stanza cut out with transcript on opposite page in Sarah Hoare's handwriting; 88–9 stanza possibly removed here (the verso of the same sheet where 41–8 have been removed); 120 the reading of the first two words of this line uncertain; 121–2 two-thirds of the leaf has been cut away, the verso of the remainder contains the following in Crabbe's hand which I quote verbatim:

> [. . . ma]ngled Limbs and flowing Blood
> Dreadful to hear and to behold
> Commanding Tears a copious Flood
> She listens in her nervous Mood
> To what she once would deeply dread
> Grieve not she Cries at Others Good
> The[?y] feel, they bleed! & they are dead

144 'in' has been inserted after 'murmuring', the line orig-
inally reading 'In murmuring miserable tone'; 159 'twice'
written over 'late'; 169–200 these four stanzas written by
Crabbe on the left-hand page, and their position in the poem
not certain; 189 'ugly' written above 'dreadful'; 201–16 these
two stanzas 'torn out' and copied in Sarah Hoare's hand; 251
'thrown' written alongside 'oergrown'; 256 alternative line
written underneath 'Who languish but who fear to die'; 264
'yet w^d' written below 'bear to'; 272–3 the deleted 'Joseph and
Jesse' stanza entered at this point (see Appendix III); 406 'this'
written above 'one'; 407 'this' written above 'One'; 408 'that'
written above 'so'; 425–32 this stanza cut out and copied in an
unidentified hand, capitalisation from 'Misery' version; 470
'To give me' written above 'That makes Life'; 491 'Is it'—the
MS reads 'Tis is'; 520–1 section headed 'Part 3rd'; 568 'curse
me if I keep' written below 'I am Cursed to keep'; 627 'grateful'
written at the end of the line; 654 'Heavn' written above 'now';
664 'think, fear feel or' written below 'feel! think! fear nor
know'; 688 'not for thee' written below 'all for me'; 709
originally 'can do' with 'can' deleted and 'do' possibly altered
to 'dost'—but it is unclear; 725 'Storm' written above 'Pang';
852 'Hope I feard to own' written above 'Wish was never
known'; 871 'that'—MS reads 'have'; 872 'pine' this may be a
mistranscription on my part; 886 'your darling boy' written
above 'an happy Boy'; 896 'sparkling' and 'Eye' written below
'reddening' and 'Cheek'; 936 'that' written above 'And'; 947
'Dogs!' written below 'Wretches!'; 960 'thus' written above
'so'; 1016 'do not' written above 'Why so' ('Why' deleted);
1021 'his' written above 'thy'; 1109 'observing' written above
'reasoning'; 1111 'first' written above 'own'; 1120 'that'
written below 'what'; 1154 'fivefold' written above 'double';
1168 'rewake Souls' written below 'wake the Soul'; 1186 'w'
written above 'No'; 1198 'flies'—MS reads 'fly'.

III. The 'Misery' verses and 'Joseph and Jesse'

The Oxford *Complete Poetical Works* publishes two drafts by
Crabbe which tie in with *The Voluntary Insane*. The most

important of these are the 'Misery' verses discussed in the Introduction, of which (for those without the Oxford edition to hand) more details are given here.

The 'Misery' draft is a fifth of the length of *The Voluntary Insane*, coming to 256 lines as against *The Voluntary Insane*'s 1206 lines. Very roughly, it corresponds to lines 57–696 of the finished text, although it contains stanzas that have later been abandoned or reworked; and the order of the stanzas has been radically altered.

To give some idea of the changes that have been made, the sequence of stanzas in the 'Misery' draft runs, according to the line-numbering of *The Voluntary Insane*, approximately as follows: 57–88, dropped stanza, 137–52, dropped stanza, 225–73, five stanzas much altered, 244–52, five stanzas much altered, 673–96, 513–20, 385–92, 417–40, 273–80, 313–20, 337–44.

The relevance of 'Joseph and Jesse' to *The Voluntary Insane* is more peripheral. It is an unfinished draft for a poem and was first published from the Murray notebooks in Arthur Pollard's *New Poems by George Crabbe* in 1960. Although it does not share the same stanza-pattern, being in quatrains rhyming *abab*, it does have some similarities to *The Voluntary Insane* in its subject matter. It tells the story of a Maiden, Jesse, who has a child out of wedlock which, it is hinted, she has murdered. She afterwards exhibits some peculiarities in her behaviour. Joseph, the narrator of the poem, is of lowly station and falls hopelessly in love with her: 'For she was Queen of all Around,/ And I the Gard'ners Helpers Boy'. In many respects, if not quite in its metre, the poem resembles a ballad.

The Oxford editors suggest that the 'Misery' verses may themselves 'be a rejected draft intended for the latter part of "Joseph and Jesse" on the subject of Jesse's madness'. This seems not to be the case—although it is impossible to be sure what Crabbe had in mind at this early stage—but it is nevertheless a shrewd guess. For there is a deleted stanza in the manuscript of *The Voluntary Insane* that shows that Crabbe did indeed at one stage have some plan of tying it in with 'Joseph and Jesse' (this falls between lines 272 and 273 of the published text):

> A young Dependant, mild and poor,
>> Had been forsaken by her Swain;
> Her Grief, though ridiculed before,
>> Now raised some Pity; for that Pain
>> She tried to ease—she would weep again,
> With Jesse weeping, and would say,
>> 'Dear Girl, you may your Peace obtain
> O! yes! for you there is a Way.'

'Joseph and Jesse' also has links with another poem in the Hoare Notebook, 'Sir Denys Banger'. Here the eponymous villain's elder brother is compared to Jesse's child. This implies that Crabbe planned to include 'Sir Denys Banger', too, as part of the sequence (see the note on dating in the Introduction). It also implies that Jesse's child was not murdered after all. Perhaps Crabbe had in mind springing a surprise reunion on us, along the lines of 'The Irish Lovers' (see Appendix IV).

IV. The Other Poems in the Hoare Notebook

The Hoare Notebook contains four poems in all. All are written in eight-line stanzas rhyming *ababbcbc*, characteristic of the 'dream poems'. They are (in order): 'Sir Denys Banger', 'The Voluntary Insane', 'The Irish Lovers', and 'The Madman's Dream'.

(i) 'Sir Denys Banger'

The original title of this (which Crabbe has not deleted) was: 'The Younger Brother/ [rule]/ There is no Peace, saith my God to the Wicked'. As far as I am aware, it is Crabbe's longest extant verse narrative. It runs to over 200 eight-line stanzas, amounting to over 1,600 lines (figures must be approximate until a proper edition is prepared). It differs from other 'dream poems' in that the lines are of ten (sometimes rising to twelve) syllables, instead of eight, while retaining the eight-line-stanza *ababbcbc* format.

Very briefly, the story tells how Denys Banger, the younger brother, disposes of his elder brother David in a canal, with the aid of a henchman called Gad. Gad flees to America. Sir Denys enjoys his inheritance. After some Byronic wanderings, Sir Denys manages to secure a wife. By this time he is suffering from terrible nightmares. His wife discovers his secret. A nameless visitor then turns up. He tells him he has learnt the secret from Gad, and Sir Denys is persuaded to make a donation towards building a church. Further visits and further donations follow. Sir Denys's beloved son—who reminds him of his murdered brother—sickens and dies. Then a seafaring beggar presents himself. He turns out to be Gad himself. Sir Denys drops dead.

A third of the way into the poem, Crabbe suddenly breaks into *ottava-rima*. It is at the point where Sir Denys has come into his ill-gotten inheritance, and, suffering from the pangs of conscience, decides to sample 'foreign Vices' (the reference to 'Bendy' is to Old Bendy, the Devil):

> And now he flies t'escape his Bosom's Pain:
> > By change of Plan, suppose we change our Style?
> His Change is oft-time made and made in vain,
> > But ours, it may be, will excite a Smile,
> Or Sooth a Reader when he feels Disdain,
> > Or is oppressed with Lassitude and Bile:
> Bendy our Verses to his view may bring—
> That is some good—a more Amusing Thing.

> Not that the Style is very hard to hit;
> > It has in truth an easy shallow flow,
> And more of idle playfulness that Wit
> > (At least than those who practice it bestow).
> It best will favoured lazy Poets fit
> > Whose Fame is granted, and whose Skill we know:
> Such will it Suit, for it indulges them
> Whom we indulged, and Care not to condemn.

The target here—the lazy, favoured, poet—is of course Lord Byron, who, with *Beppo* and, above all, *Don Juan*, had made this verse-form his own.

Byron greatly admired Crabbe. His tribute to the older poet from his *English Bards and Scotch Reviewers* is engraved—marred by a slight misquotation (unless the text given in the *Life* is at fault)—on Crabbe's funeral monument at Trowbridge:

AS A WRITER, HE IS WELL DESCRIBED BY A GREAT
CONTEMPORARY AS
'NATURE'S STERNEST PAINTER, YET HER [*sic*] BEST.'

Byron swore that 'Crabbe's the man', and that he and the banker-poet Samuel Rogers were 'the fathers of present Poesy' (letters to John Murray, 15 September 1817 and 2 February 1818). However, in terms of popularity, it was Byron who was by then the man. The peak of Crabbe's popularity, the publication of his *Verse Tales* in 1812 (which ran through three editions), coincided with Byron's meteoric rise. Thereafter it was Byron who set the fashion.

In financial terms, Crabbe's success reached its acme in December 1818 when he abandoned John Hatchard of Piccadilly and went over to Byron's publisher, John Murray, who purchased his previous copyrights for an enormous £3,000—a sum equal to the advance paid by Longmans for Moore's *Lalla Rookh* (1817), then the highest sum ever paid for a poem.

But Crabbe was already, in terms of popularity, over the hill. Murray brought out Crabbe's *Tales of the Hall* on 3 July 1819. It was a great critical success. But it did not sell. A few years later it was remaindered, and it is calculated that Murray, who had paid out large sums on illustrations, lost about £2,500 on the deal.

On 15 July 1819, a fortnight after publication of the *Tales of the Hall*, Murray also brought out the first two Cantos of Byron's *Don Juan*. It met the opposite fate. The critics damned it, and it sold in enormous quantities.

Murray had been a reluctant publisher of *Don Juan*, and

Crabbe evidently shared his misgivings. Word of this reached Byron, who complained to Murray: 'You are right—Gifford is right—Crabbe is right—Hobhouse is right—You are all right—and I am all wrong—but do pray let me have that pleasure . . .' (12 August 1819).

By a small stroke of irony, Crabbe was one of those singled out for praise in Byron's Dedication to *Don Juan*, where Wordsworth and the Lakers are told that 'Scott, Rogers, Campbell, Moore, and Crabbe, will try/ 'Gainst you the question with posterity'. But Crabbe may not have seen this (unless Murray showed it him in manuscript), as the Dedication was suppressed and circulated in pirate broadsheet only. He would however have seen the reference to himself at the end of the first Canto:

> Thou shalt believe in Milton, Dryden, Pope;
>   Thou shalt not set up Wordsworth, Coleridge, Southey;
> Because the first is crazed beyond all hope,
>   The second drunk, the third so quaint and mouthy;
> With Crabbe it may be difficult to cope,
>   And Campbell's Hippocrene is somewhat drouthy:
> Thou shalt not steal from Samuel Rogers, nor
> Commit—flirtation with the muse of Moore.
>
> (Canto I, ccv)

Poetasters might have found it difficult to cope with Crabbe; but Crabbe did not find it difficult to cope with Byron. In all, thirty-six stanzas of 'Sir Denys Banger' are written in the Don's metre. After recounting the seduction by Sir Denys of a mother and her daughter—'A fouler Deed Men said was never acted/ Her daughter lived, the Mother died distracted'—Crabbe rams the point home:

> In fact Sir Denys much resembled One
>   Childe Harold, with whom all Men are Acquainted:
> True, of his Race, a smaller Part was run,
>   Yet Life to him with darker Hue was painted—
> He had done more!—yet not so much had done,
>   And, less experienced, was more deeply tainted;
> An eager Man, who through the World would ramble,
> And for its Treasures and Enjoyments scramble.

Sir Denys fled, pursued by Hate and Curses,
    To Greece, where soft voluptuous Ease man blesses:
But of this Leisure nought the Muse rehearses,
    Save that he sought young maids with jetty tresses,
With Eyes that cannot be described by Verses,
    With Elegance in all their Steps and Dresses—
Of these he purchased a Sufficient Number,
To make the will, but not the Conscience, slumber.

'Sir Denys Banger' is not a very good poem, but it is a potent literary curiosity.

(ii) 'The Voluntary Insane'

This follows after 'Sir Denys Banger', and in its turn is followed by 'The Irish Lovers'.

(iii) 'The Irish Lovers'

'The Irish Lovers', like 'The Voluntary Insane', is written in the dream-poem format, although it has some introductory stanzas written in octosyllabic rhyming couplets. The introduction comes to nearly 90 lines, the tale itself to 336 lines (42 stanzas), amounting in all to about 420 lines.

The story tells of two maidens:

My Jane and I had Sister-Minds,
    We dwelt by Liffy's limpid flood . . .

They fall in love with each other's brother. The Narrator is the unlucky one. Her friend Jane manages, after some opposition, to get married; while the Narrator's match to Jane's brother is forbidden. Jane gets pregnant and gloats. The Narrator, still unmarried, unfortunately follows her example ('my altered form disclosed my state'). The Narrator has her baby. This does not please her brother, who murders the child's father (his own brother-in-law). The Narrator's child is taken from her. Like Ellen Orford, she seeks consolation in school-teaching ('I now became of Use and taught/ The Peasant Girls for many a Year'). Jane dies and the Narrator's brother, the murderer, falls on hard times. This leads to a reconciliation. In the last couplet we discover what we have long anticipated. The Narrator, like Charlotte Brontë's improbable Mrs Pryor, has been telling her story to her daughter all along, the last lines of the poem being:

> For she that darling Child art thou
> And that afflicted Mother—I.—.'

(iv) 'The Madman's Dream'

'The Madman's Dream' is an expanded version of the dream-poem 'The Insanity of Ambitious Love', first published in 1960 from a notebook in the John Murray archive.

The latter is described by Terence Bareham as being 'perhaps the most extraordinary of all the poems in this group', and by Alethea Hayter as:

> One of the most wonderful of Crabbe's studies of madness, a detailed portrait of schizophrenia, with its vanity, its shiftiness and its pathos . . . a penetrating psychological study—as in the case of Peter Grimes but in a different direction—Crabbe developed a tendency of his own personality, which his opium dreams had pointed out to him, to its extreme, and embodied it in a madman. It has a curious kinship with Baudelaire's *La Chambre Double* . . .

In 'The Madman's Dream' the introduction runs to about 200 lines. In the published version it runs to 43. The main body of the poem, in which the dream is recounted, comes in 'The Madman's Dream' to about 480 lines, in the published version to about 380. In total, 'The Madman's Dream' has about 260 extra lines. The openings of both versions are written in rhyming couplets, and the main body in the eight-line stanza dream-poem format.

The introduction sets the scene for the opium-induced dream to follow. The dreamer of 'The Madman's Dream' is described as suffering from a Malvolio complex, after having entered the service of a 'Countess (younger than her Lord)'. He had previously been employed in a cloth-mill, where his father was clerk.

The description of this cloth mill probably recalls a visit made by Crabbe to the Doncaster works of his friend Edmund Cartwright, pioneer of the power-loom, in the summer of 1787:

> Clerk was that Father in a vast Concern,
> Where One huge Wheel ten thousand Spindles turn;
> And minor wheels, for many a Curious Use
> Their sundry Motions and Effects, produce
> Huge Bales of Cotton, as they thither come,
> Pass from the whirling Spindle to the Loom!—
> Pass from the loom, till, in new form and Dye,
> On the fair Maid they draw th'approving Eye . . .

The core of the opium-inspired dream remains the same in both versions, although in 'The Madman's Dream' Crabbe's devastating vision of factory and office life during the Industrial Revolution has been slightly expanded.

Often what Crabbe does is to take one stanza and split it into two, expanding each half into a full-length stanza (a technique akin to dividing plants). The following extract from 'The Madman's Dream' corresponds to lines 215–27 of the published version:

> At length we stopped: about the Cave
>   Was heard a Storm; the Wind was cold!
> Men viewless mourned as o'er the Grave;
>   And distant Bells were for them tolled!
>   Wild Birds screamed, and the rocks around:
> Wild Waves beat on the sounding Shore;
>   And many a nameless Sullen Sound
> Seemed some strange Evil to deplore.
>
> Light stole upon a far-spread Plain,
>   Bare-trodden!—Worn on every side;
> And there Men wrought with ceaseless Pain,
>   And to their cruel Tasks applied:
>   Their Wool they combed, they span, they dyed—
> All deadly pale, and Woe begone!—
>   They took some paltry pay and sighed—
> 'This, this, the Meed by Labour won!'

My silent Guide her Grief expressed
  By gentle pity's softest sigh;
But not a Word to me addressed:
  She judged, I could myself apply
  The View of Woe that pained the Eye—
Sad Lesson!—And I turned to look
  On all who suffering wished to die;
By Labour worn, by Terror shook.

Pale Clerks were writing on their Seats,
  With faces full of care and wan;
Some slowly sought their poor Retreats,
  Where the sad Wife received her Man
  In silence, or some Tale began
Of the unvaried Woe; and some
  From the domestic sorrow ran,
And fled the melancholy Home.

Even though it may not revolutionise our perception of his achievement in the way that I believe *The Voluntary Insane* does, 'The Madman's Dream' is an important addition to the Crabbe canon.

V. A Leaf at the Royal College of Surgeons

Some stray lines by Crabbe were first published in the Oxford *Complete Poetical Works* under the heading '[Enclosed in a Letter to Sarah Hoare]'. The letter in question is by Crabbe and is postmarked from Trowbridge, 3 September 1825. For a while I thought that this might provide evidence for dating *The Voluntary Insane*.

The verses, written in dream-poem format, begin:

Another tells a Tale of Richard Smith,
A Smith by Trade, and how he made a Shoe . . .   (1-2)

and ramble on for forty-eight lines about what sort of poem Crabbe should try his hand at. They include the lines:

I rather hear a Tale of Robin Hood,
  Clim of the Clough and William Cloudesley;
Rather the pretty Children of the Wood
Than puzzled by involved Narration be . . .   (33-6)

At the beginning of 'Sir Denys Banger', on the recto of the
third leaf of the Hoare Notebook, Crabbe has deleted some
lines with a diagonal stroke:

> Then let me read a Tale of Robin Hood
> Clim of the Clough and William Cloudesley;
> Nay let me hear the Children of the Wood—
> They Puzzle not, although they please not me . . .

Facing these verses in the notebook is a jagged stub, where a
leaf has been cut out with what appear to be sewing scissors.

The manuscript of the verses published in the Oxford
Complete Poetical Works and the accompanying letter are in the
Hunter-Baillie Collection, held at the Royal College of
Surgeons, Lincoln's Inn Fields, London. This is a collection
partly formed by the playwright Joanna Baillie, a Hampstead
neighbour and friend of Sarah Hoare's.

The Hunter-Baillie verses are written on two sides of a
ruled single leaf. The jagged edge of the leaf and the stub
remaining in the notebook match exactly, as do the feint lines
ruled in pencil and red crayon; and part of a diagonal
cancellation stroke in ink extends from the leaf onto the
corresponding page in the notebook. There can be no doubt
that the leaf was cut from the notebook.

The letter mounted with the leaf is in fact a fragment cut
from the bottom of an autograph letter written by Crabbe to
Sarah Hoare. It is fairly obvious that it has been cut by Sarah
Hoare herself, in order to furnish Joanna Baillie with an
example of the poet's signature (it is similar in this respect to
the cutting pasted into Ellen Toller's copy of the 1834 *Life*
mentioned in the Introduction). There is no evidence to
suggest that the leaf was ever enclosed in the letter; indeed,
as the leaf shows no sign of ever having been folded, this
possibility does not exist. The date of the letter is therefore a
red herring, and has no bearing on the date of the verses.

VI. *An Anonymous Letter*

On the fly-leaf of the Hoare Notebook is an extract written in
Crabbe's hand and subscribed 'Letter Aug. 1819'. I do not

know who wrote the original letter, or about whom it is written. It is possible that it was written by one of the Hoare family about Wordsworth, who, like Crabbe, often used their house as a London base on his visits from the northern fastness of Grasmere. But this is only a guess, and the date of the letter does not tie in with any of Wordsworth's visits to Heath House. It could have been written by anyone about anyone (although of sufficient interest to Crabbe to warrant the effort of writing it down):

> The Expectation of M^r W's—'He evidently expected more of us than he found—He did not feel the Interval as we did—Ours had been filled up by many Occurrances/ many Engagements, many Attentions. He had never been interupted in his Thoughts of us, by Anything which interfered with his Affectn/ therefore he came expecting the Joy of Gratulation which He Could not find, certainly not in the Degree expected by him & we, our Minds preoccupied, found not that Desire of listening to & being entertained by him which he in his Affection nothing abated, certainly looked for.—Letter Aug. 1819.

Bibliography and Abbreviations

Bareham   Terence Bareham, *George Crabbe*, 1977

Broadley   A. M. Broadley and Walter Jerrold, *The Romance of an Elderly Poet*, 1913

CH   *Crabbe: the Critical Heritage*, 1972, edited by Arthur Pollard

CPW   George Crabbe, *The Complete Poetical Works*, 3 vols, 1988, edited by Norma Dalrymple-Champneys and Arthur Pollard

Hayter   Alethea Hayter, *Opium and the Romantic Imagination*, 1968

Hoare   *Memoirs of Samuel Hoare by his Daughter Sarah and his Widow Hannah*, 1911, edited by F. R. Pryor

Huchon   René Huchon, *George Crabbe and his Times*, 1907

Index   *Index of English Literary Manuscripts*, vol. iii, pt. i, 1968, 'George Crabbe', compiled by Margaret M. Smith

L&J   George Crabbe, *Selected Letters and Journals*, 1985, edited by Thomas C. Faulkner and Rhonda L. Blair

Life   *The Poetical Works of the Rev. George Crabbe with his Letters and Journals and his Life*, 1834, vol. i, the *Life* by George Crabbe Jr.

Munby   A. N. L. Munby, *The Cult of the Autograph Letter in England*, 1962

NP   *New Poems by George Crabbe*, 1960, edited by Arthur Pollard

Wordsworth   William Wordsworth, *Poetical Works*, vol. iv, 1947, edited by E. de Selincourt and Helen Darbishire

References

Introduction

Page

10	original, vigorous, elegant	*CH* 41
12	The late Dr. Club	*Life* 161
14	The influence of opium on Crabbe's verse	*CPW* i 602–3
15	a tramp, tramp, tramp	*CH* 368
15	Nature's sternest painter	*CH* 294
15	next Mrs Crabbe	*CH* 295
15	describes the interior	*CH*213
15	an absolute defect	*CH* 298
15	in addition to great powers	*CH* 296
15	Crabbe was not a poet	*CH* 485
16	we have repeatedly expressed	*CH* 384
16	during the hotter months	*Life* 163
17	Crabbe himself wrote	*CPW* iii 476n
17	some time before Mr Crabbe	*Life* 36n
17	that of the first-rate yeoman	*Life* 142
18	a fine hale girl	*Life* 40
18	I have heard my father	*Life* 40–1
19	I had long	*L&J* xxv
20	spreading in the same neighbourhood	*Life* 181–2
21	so large a portion	*Life* 211
22	I was incommoded	*Life* 253; *L&J* 221
23	his dead wife	see also *L&J* 221 n72
23	Terence Bareham	Bareham 58
24	surrounding moat	*Life* 142
24	determined to go	*Life* 42
24	a sweet little villa	*Life* 147; Huchon 71–2
25	as if by instinct	*Life* 145–6
26	According to Crabbe's later biographer	Huchon 54, 420–2
27	It was first published	*CPW* iii 475–82
29	This is inscribed	*Index* 295
29	when, eighty years later	*CPW* i, xxviii

REFERENCES

WILBERFORCE BUXTON CANNING LUSHI...

CAMPBELL BYRON CRABBE

ERSKINE MRS SIDDONS

MRS FRY

SAMUEL HOARE
DIED 1825